25ᵗʰ Anniversary Edition

SING & COOK
with
ANDY LORUSSO,
THE SINGING CHEF®

25th Anniversary Edition

SING & COOK
with
ANDY LORUSSO
THE SINGING CHEF®

Special Bonus Section: Sing Along Songs & Recipes
Global Adventures & Foods

*Now everyone can sing while they cook a great meal with
Andy! Just go to the links and download the song you want
to sing, pour the wine, and let the magic begin!
Engage All Your Senses!*

Happy Heart Publishing
Santa Barbara, CA
2017

For information, write to:
Happy Heart Publishing
PO Box 91725
Santa Barbara, CA 93190

ISBN: 978-0-692-90871-6

Credits:
Author photo, front cover: Chumash Casino staff photographer
Author photos, back cover and interior: Darrel Westmorland
Food photos: Jim Zhan
Assistant to Mr. Zhan: Airi Ikeda
Drawn illustrations: Lucinda Rea, http://lucinda-rae.com
Editing, cover design, and interior design: Teresa Lynn, www.henscratches.com

Back cover food recipes:
Crostini with Gorgonzola, Roasted Peppers, and Balsamic Glaze, page 24
Nonna Grace's Sicilian Ricotta Cheesecake, page 125
Turkey Bolognese with Pappardelle, page 80

This book is dedicated not only to my loving family,
from whom I inherited my love of food and music,
but to my world family,
who have supported my passion to celebrate all cultures
with a commonality that brings us all together.

To my teachers of the divine truth
who have guided me along the way with their ancient wisdom
and taught me how to tap into that still, quiet place within my heart
to witness the joy of living!
Tutto Amore!

Best wishes
Mary Chase

Table of Contents

My father's LoRusso family, approximately 1937 in Upper Greenwood Lake, NJ
Standing in rear (left to right): my father Andrew, Uncle Bill, Grandpa Angelo, Uncle Joe
Sitting in front (left to right): Pal the German Shepherd, Uncle Angelo, Uncle Anthony,
Aunt Beatrice, Grandma Mary, Uncle Salvatore (Chippy)

Foreword

With great pleasure I compose this foreword to the new edition of *Sing and Cook Italian*. I have known my cousin, Andy LoRusso, my whole life but most particularly in our adulthood for the last 24 years since I moved to Los Angeles, exactly 100 miles from his home in Santa Barbara, a drive on the 101 that he and I know well. Our time spent together has been spent singing Beach Boys harmonies, discussing the ancient Indian Vedic texts he has mastered, drinking wine, cooking, and sharing our experiences with people and places all around the world. The core of our experience is our reverence for our grandfather and grandmother, the parents of my mother Beatrice and his father Andrew. This new edition of *Sing and Cook* roots itself in this very experience of family.

More than a cookbook in the practical sense, the new edition takes a broader, more capacious approach to the concepts of song, food, cooking, and family. It chronicles various experiences of the Singing Chef® as he meets people, enters new environments, encounters new cultures, and explores the nexus between song and food globally. To sing and to cook are more than two types of exuberance, though indeed they are that, for they manifest two of the highest expressions of human art and imagination. They also reveal how human beings can come together in the deepest sense of celebrating joy and the purpose of life. To eat is to sustain existence; to cook is to sustain something less tangible but equally urgent—a way of preserving culture, nostalgia, relationships, traditions, the ways of the past that make us who we are and allow us to cherish a cultural identity that we can share with others.

I can't think of anyone more qualified to present these experiences and to guide the reader through these recipes and these cultural encounters. My cousin, of course raised in the rich Italian Catholic tradition of our ancestors, has been practitioner of Transcendental Meditation and a student of ancient Indian philosophy for the last 45 years. Quite amazingly, along with the Beach Boys and the Beatles he was also a student and an associate of the Maharishi, from whom he acquired his mantra. A trained musician his whole life himself, he's sensitive to Indian music, Italian folksongs music and all the chants and percussive sounds from everywhere he has traveled, performed and cooked. The philosophy of this book maintains that singing will bring people together by calming their hearts and restoring something lost in the technological society of today, something that harkens back to a simpler, pre-scientific and pre-industrial past, something at the core of all the families and all the human hearts around the world. If this sounds somewhat sentimental, it is, since sentiment, the realization that the "other" feels as we do, brings and keeps people together, transcending difference and melting fear of the unknown. By disposition, training, and through the great spiritual gifts he has been given and has acquired in his travels, Andy LoRusso is uniquely able to offer to the reading public this volume of recipes, reminiscences, and family experiences—from New Jersey to California and all the way to Istanbul. In song and in food we find more than just entertainment and cuisine. We find that connection to each other as we come to understand our shared sense of humanity.

So I welcome the readers to this volume and hope that it provides the same sense of joy and the same opportunity for harmony and peace that I myself have experienced in our Italian family ever since our grandfather, Angelo LoRusso, first came to this country almost a hundred years ago, not speaking the language, with a dollar in his pocket so to speak, and with the hope of making a new future for himself. He used to tell us that in Potenza in southern Italy where he was born, people were so poor that they lived on *pane e cippole* (bread and onions). I've always imagined that even in the simplicity of this rustic, peasant fare, well-earned with their intense daily labors, they found a deep sense of community and unity among each other which sustained their feelings of hope for the future. Our grandfather could never have imagined a book like this being written a hundred years after his voyage across the Atlantic, but I'm sure he would be deeply proud if he could see what has sprung from the seed that he planted with his courage and his sacrifice.

Michael Calabrese
Professor of English
California State University, Los Angeles

About Andy LoRusso, The Singing Chef®

ANDY LoRusso, KNOWN the world over as The Singing Chef®, gained fame when he published his iconic book *Sing & Cook Italian*, which led to a full-time career traveling around the country and the world performing his interactive singing & cooking shows. He has been seen not only on national TV (see his appearance on *The Donny & Marie Show* on YouTube), but also in major theaters, festivals, casinos, and at charitable fundraisers. Thousands of happy people have sung along with him and tasted his amazing foods, originating from his Italian (Neapolitan and Sicilian) family.

Since his childhood growing up in Newark, New Jersey, Andy has had a gift for creating a party atmosphere with his love for family, food, and song. He signed with Epic records in his early 20s, singing Rhythm & Blues and Soul with some of the top musicians of the time. You can listen to his hit single *The Great Magic of Love*, now a cult classic, and the flip side, *Dancing Master*, on his YouTube channel.

Along the way, Andy had the good fortune to meet and study with one of the premier operatic vocal coaches. The singers of old, in jazz, opera, and pop, inspired him to learn both the arias and the love songs that he grew up listening to at the apron strings of his Grandmother Grace, in her simple but soulful kitchen, while she cooked. In 1991, Andy invented a way to combine his passion for music and food by cooking his family's best recipes to classic, beautiful love songs, and The Singing Chef® was born!

This cookbook now gives the links to his *That's Amore* CD—the perfect musical complement to cooking a romantic dinner or a celebration with family and friends. It is also filled with great recipes for foods and recommendations for wines that Andy has discovered in his world travels. Find it on Amazon.com at the following link: https://www.amazon.com/gp/product/B06Y2K1PBD/ref=dm_ws_sp_ps_dp

In the bonus section of this cookbook, everyone can now learn to sing along with Andy, as they assemble the ingredients to some of the most loved recipes from Italy, France, Mexico, and from all around the world.

To learn where Andy is performing, try more recipes, and discover his music, explore his website, http://www.SingingChef.com. You can also follow Andy on Facebook, LinkedIn, Google +, and Instagram by searching for Andy LoRusso, The Singing Chef®.

Buon appetito!

Acknowledgments

FIRST OF ALL, I would like to give thanks to some of the loving people that have been in my life for these past years, for without their love and support I would not have ventured out in the world with this new project: Bill and Jill Spencer and family, Dr. Frankie "The Wrench" DiChiara, Don & Etta Nicewonder, and others too numerous to mention. Many thanks to Professor Michael Calabrese, my dear cousin, who gave me some important background on our family history and who shares my love of family, food, wine, and all things Italian. Most of all, thanks to my bother Ronald and his wife Bobbie, and my significant other, Nena Spencer, whom I first met on Polkaerobics, another project I created in 1987. She became my dance partner, and for the last 25-plus years has kept me dancing on a roller coaster ride of emotions, fueled by her love of art, writing, music, and the real truth of being alive.

I would also like to acknowledge some of the stellar chefs and supporters I've met and worked with along the way: Jim and Tina Aho, Joe Baumel, Dan Catanio, Joe Edem, Richard Fisher, Joe Font, Tony Gemignani, Anna Lopez-Car, Donatella Lopez-Le Sorelle, Etta Nicewonder, Brad Sherman, Asif Rasheed Syed, and Darrell Westmoreland. They will always be tops in my book.

Add some music to your day. ~The Beach Boys

Singing for My Supper

The Secret Ingredient Is the Singing

THE TITLE OF this book pretty much tells it all. My career as The Singing Chef® has been pure magic. Not only am I singing for my supper, but for breakfast, lunch, dinner, and between-meal espressos, too.

I never thought that I would create a full-time career doing what I have a passion for: singing, cooking, eating, and traveling the world. But with the publication of my first cookbook and CD, *Sing and Cook Italian*, I have done just that. It's good when we can engage all of our senses in the experience.

I have come a long way from the very first R&B single I recorded for Epic records back in the late 60s under the name of Palmer Jones. (Listen to both *The Great Magic of Love* and *Dancing Master* on YouTube.) The writers of a few hit songs of that time, Sandy Linzer and Denny Randell, thought my voice was like Tom Jones. He and BJ Thomas were topping the charts back then. The two songs they chose for me to sing were in that same category of rhythm and blues, and soul.

Along the way, I have had many small miracles. The one I was totally blown away by was finding my only child, Betty Hoops, who had been given up for adoption; and then finding out that she is a graduate of the Culinary Institute of America. A chef! Now that's pure magic. (You can read the full story, *Together Again*, on the "About Andy" page of my website, www.singingchef.com; and see her website at www.bettyhoops.com.)

In traveling the globe, I have experienced some delicious foods and wines. That inspired me to create some of my signature Italian recipes, and to share those dishes, along with others that I have cooked and eaten along the way. These are recipes, food, and songs that I have eaten and shared with family and friends in a number of different countries.

The internet and social networking have been a big help in getting the message out that singing and music can be an integral part of the dining experience, setting a happy mood—and the happiness goes into the food. From my private client parties, to large ballrooms in casinos and hotels, and on the stage of some historical theaters, I share good food and good music.

My very first national TV exposure with Donny and Marie Osmond also gave my Nonna Grace's Ricotta Cheesecake—for which we all sang the ingredients on air (see video on YouTube)—a nationwide and loyal following. It's simple and easy to make.

In my cookbook *Sing and Cook Italian*, published in 1993, I talk about my family on my mother's side, and all the memories of her kitchen and the special holidays for which she cooked great homemade Italian meals for everyone. She would from time to time play the music of some of the great tenors and sopranos of the golden age of opera, and also well-known Italian popular singers like my cousin Phil Brito, whose songs, along with Mario Lanza's, were on the top of the charts in her house.

I believe in the importance of getting back to the habit of the family cooking and eating together, to generate more harmony and have face-to-face conversations with each other, not just on the cell phones and internet as we have now. Eating in a quiet, settled environment will aid in the digestion process, as has been scientifically proven. Using seasonal foods that enhance the dish you are cooking while also supporting the local farmers markets as much as possible to assure the freshest ingredients is a good start.

Food from the Land of Song

In Italy, everybody sings! From the people on the street and the workers in the fields to the city dwellers and businesspeople, everybody sings. That's why it's called the "land of song."

Italy's is a rich culture, filled with music and song. Everywhere you look, you find a work of art. Italians themselves are a work of art, and this is exemplified especially in their food.

The neighborhood I grew up in was like that. We would sing on the street corners and in the tunnels around the city. We would sing *a cappella* (unaccompanied) and people would gather around and sometimes join in. There was always a pizzeria close by, and the smell of fresh garlic and tomatoes would stir our taste buds and inspire us to sing more.

Sometimes, one of the boys would want to impress a girl, and our group of singers would gather outside her house, under her window, and sing love songs. The girl being serenaded would eventually stick her head out the window and throw a kiss to us – but not before her father would tell us to move on or he would call the police!

We sang at all the family picnics and the weddings. My uncle's band would play the standard Italian songs and we, not always understanding the words, would sing along, having a great time anyway. I remember the weddings as being like those in *The Godfather*—everyone would dance and sing for as long as the band played.

When I was in the fifth grade, I was asked to get up in front of the class and sing one of the popular songs, "Teenager in Love." I felt shy standing there, so I put on my best smile and pretended to be on a street corner. I did so well that they asked me to sing again on the bus during a field trip. I never forgot the experience. I've always won people over with a song whenever I got the chance.

Singing opens up a whole new world. Try it. It doesn't matter what anyone says or thinks, just do it. Whatever comes out is divine. The more you sing, the more confidence you achieve; and, before you know it, you'll be right up there on stage with the best of them.

Food: The Gift of Love

Growing up in an Italian neighborhood in New Jersey was like living in Italy. The Italian food market on the way to school always had some magical, alluring aroma emanating from its doors. I would be drawn into its spell and, once inside, be filled with the smells of fresh parmesan and romano cheese balls hanging in the window. The sight of fresh mozzarella cheese (and I mean the kind where the milk is oozing out of it, not the rubbery kind you find in the supermarket) was enough to make my mouth water. This is not to mention the rows of freshly-made pasta and the barrels of olives. The sausage was made fresh every day and would hang in the case where the pastas were.

The bread was fresh from the Italian bakery down the street, and that alone would make me want to stop and buy everything in the store. I remember that bakery on the way to church or school. Every morning it was filled with people buying up everything in the store. You had to get there early for some breads. I always ate the ends before I got home. They were delicious!

I grew up on 100-percent Italian food. My mother, a first-generation Italian-American, learned to cook from her mother, Grace, who was born in Agira in eastern Sicily. My father, also a first-generation American, learned to cook from his mother, who was born in southern Italy, in the region of Potenza. I loved to listen to my grandfather's stories of when he was a young boy. His family had a farm on which they raised goats and chickens—fresh eggs, cheese, and milk every day. Their vegetables came right out of their garden.

Hard work, family, and lots of time together: It was simple life with simple pleasures. My Grandmother Grace would listen to the operas every chance she had. I was exposed to the great singers as my grandmother listened to the great music while cooking. The music, the voices,and the orchestras are ingrained in my bones forever.

There is a definite link between food and family in Italy. Food shared at the table is a gift of love, a way of showing others how much you care for them and their health. I feel that this is one of the reasons that the family group remains so strong with Italians. There isn't a day that goes by that Italians don't talk about food. We talk about the next meal while we're eating the one before us! Food is an Italian's way of giving love from the heart.

There are many different types of cooking in Italy. Each region has its own specialties and methods of preparation. Northern, central, and southern Italy are broken into 23 regions, each with its own culture, dialect, and food. *Mangia* ("eat") is a magic word; I learned it from Grandmother Grace, who was always ready to open the refrigerator and cook a meal for anyone who walked into her kitchen. "*Dio ti benedici* (God bless you)," she would say, and start cooking.

My Father's Side of the Family

When you travel back to the ancient *paese*, to the land of your ancestors, to find your *radici* (roots), and meet cousins and extended family members that you never knew, amazingly, and almost miraculously, you realize that you have really found a part of yourself. All personal histories, separated by oceans and time, dissolve and reemerge into a greater sense of family and tradition. They know you, and you know them, without a word needing to be spoken. Once you see them, face to face, you are home. All that remains then is, of course, to cook.

My grandfather Angelo Michele LoRusso came to America as a teenager. He was only 19 years old. His brothers Joe and Robert (my uncles—Zio Pepe and Zio Antonio, as they are known in our family), came to America before him and sent back word to Italy that they had a very nice girl for him to marry. She lived in the boarding house where they first lived with other people from the same village in Italy. That's how Grandfather Angelo LoRusso came to America and ended up marrying Mary Incoronata Romano, whose name honors the Virgin Mary, "enthroned" as queen of heaven. They had seven children: six boys and one girl. Andrew, my father, who always cooked in our house when my mother was working, was a war hero. He was given the Purple Heart for injury he received as a soldier on the field of battle in the European theater during WWII, and came home to us with honors. My uncles William (Bill), Anthony, Joseph, Salvatore, and Angelo, along with my Aunt Beatrice, made up the rest of grandfather's family.

My grandmother Mary died at a young age in 1949, and we had our grandfather move in with us in Newark, New Jersey. He shared stories with me of growing up on a small farm in Avigliano, in the province of Potenza, located in southern Italy. The high, rough mountains made agriculture difficult, and a long history of disease, disaster, poverty, and struggle led, in one of the most important events in world history, to the vast migration of millions of Southern Italians to America, leaving behind desperation and hardship for a new opportunity to provide for their families and to create a future that they knew would be denied them in Italy. The new struggles, in language, culture, and assimilation, would present a new set of woes and anxieties; but as new Americans, these Italian immigrants fought proudly for their families and for their new nation, and they proudly preserved the ancient religion, family, and, as is crucial to the survival of the Italian way, food. Simple, tasteful, and filled with love were the foods that they served, both in everyday survival and on the days of feast and celebration, around the table for hours, with wine, stories, and remembrances.

A Festival in the Kitchen

I love going to ethnic festivals, and especially entertaining at them. Food, song, and dance seem to go together very well. I find myself transported to whatever country is being fêted—France, Spain, Greece, Italy. It becomes a trip around the world.

Cooking, too, is like a festival in your own kitchen. Invite all your family and friends, and have them sing and cook with you. The food, you'll find, tastes better. We need to get back to where we all eat together more often. It's hard in this era of two-family income earners, when we're all running helter-skelter and eating on the run, to enjoy a home-cooked meal. Our fixation on fast food is not good for our digestion. We need to slow down, set apart some time each week to get together with family and friends, and sing and cook a great meal.

***

Eating is a spiritual experience, and the food we eat becomes us. (Sound familiar?) One of the most important things in the preparation of good food, as well as eating it, is one's frame of mind. It's essential to be relaxed in both mind and body, and that's where singing helps. A good frame of mind lets us enjoy our food and digest it better, getting the maximum nutrition from it. Good conversation, a relaxed environment, and joyful thoughts all lend to a great meal. Smells are also important; just smelling your food, the digestive process starts immediately. It's important to use only fresh ingredients, spices, and seasonings in your cooking. A simple life—eat, sing, and be happy.

This book is written to help us get the most out of life in each moment. It is dedicated to all those lovers of *romanza*, good food, and good times—to my family, aunts, uncles, cousins, and friends, who have shared their love with me at the dinner table and get-togethers all over the country. *Lasciamo che la morte ci trovi pieni di vita*! Let death find us filled with life!

I would like this book, with its songs and recipes, to bring a little bit of fun and celebration to all who use it. I am grateful to all my teachers, friends, lovers, and guardian angels who have traveled with me this far, and all those who are yet to come.

The Main Course; or, Feed Me and I'll Follow You Anywhere

The main characteristic of Italian cooking is its healthy balance: basic ingredients are cooked simply and retain their original goodness and freshness. This simplicity is linked to such a variety of flavors and rich inventiveness in preparation that the gourmet is delighted. If you would like to sample all kinds of cooking, you should go not only to the well-known restaurants that feature regional cuisine (Tuscany, Bologna, Emilia, Rome, Naples, etc.), but to the modest *trattorie*, which are more home-like and where they are proud to have you taste their specialties. You should dine at restaurants where, weather permitting, you can eat outdoors. The hours passed under a *pergola* or on a sunlit terrace bright with the colors of curtains and parasols, gazing out over a landscape of green and gold, can be some of the most beautiful, romantic memories made in Italy.

Eating Italian the Weight-Conscious Way

It's important to clear up the myth of the Italian diet. Many people associate Italian cuisine with over-indulgence and see themselves only gaining weight. Italian food is "indulgent" because it's delicious, with lush textures and flavors, but its reputation for putting on pounds is undeserved.

The nutritional foundation of Italian food is pasta, a complex carbohydrate. It takes longer to digest than the simple carbohydrates, such as sugar. Pasta's benefits are twofold: (1) your body receives the energy-giving sugar at a steady rate, avoiding the crash-and-burn blood-sugar cycle of simple carbohydrates; and (2) you stay sated for a longer time. This is good for those physically active people who need lots of reserve fuel.

What one puts on the pasta, however, is what can put on the weight. If you're weight conscious, look for light, oil-based sauces that are tossed with herbs, seafood, or vegetables, and fresh garden tomatoes. Olive oil is a great nutritional plus: this monounsaturated fat is credited with helping lower the cholesterol level in the blood.

A word about pizza: Italian connoisseurs watching their waistlines can enjoy pizza. It's an excellent opportunity for a nutritional meal. It helps to choose the ingredients carefully. Whole-wheat and whole-grain crust and low-fat or skim-milk mozzarella is a plus, as are vegetables like peppers, mushrooms, broccoli, artichoke hearts, and—my favorite—olives and sun-dried tomatoes Yes, you can enjoy pizza without guilt.

Preparing for the Italian Dinner

The subject, singing and cooking (especially Italian), is close to my heart. I've met few people who would turn down a great Italian dinner, no matter the season. And I've met few people who would object to a love song or two before, during, or after a meal.

When I sing while cooking, I'm put in a particular state of mind, like traveling in Italy—floating down the river in a gondola with someone special, or high on a mountain overlooking the azure-blue Mediterranean. The beautiful Italian melodies conjure up visions of an accordion, a sweet violin, or a grand piano that go tenderly and directly to my heart—and into the food I'm preparing.

When considering which recipes to include, I went right to the storehouse of the family treasures: my aunts, my mother, and my grandmother, Grace, who cooked with a pinch of this and a shake of that. When she was growing up, there was no refrigeration, so everything was prepared fresh, right from the garden. The pasta was made by hand with fresh ingredients and put into the sun to dry. Vegetables were picked just before being used, and the sauces cooked for hours.

The Italian Dinner

The dinner table at my house was always a place of great joy, especially around the holidays like Christmas. Grandmother Grace and all her children would help her prepare a twelve-course feast, everything from soup to nuts. The dinner would start with different types of fish (Sicily is a great seaport), influenced by the "catch of the day": *baccala* (cod), dried and breaded; *calamari* (squid) stuffed with crab or lobster; raw shrimp in a garlic-butter sauce; mussels in marinara; crabs in season served in marinara with *capillini* (angel hair) pasta. One of my favorite holiday dishes was Pasta Mudica, a long tube-type pasta served with sardines, olive oil, and seasoned bread crumbs. Always, there would be parmesan and romano cheeses and, of course, fresh bread.

Then came the pastas: gnocchi, a type of dumpling served with vegetables; cavatelli and fresh broccoli; clams and linguine; ravioli with marinara; and, sometimes, lasagna with lots of mozzarella cheese.

The dessert trays were filled with the most colorful assortment of cookies and pastries you could imagine. Cannoli, *sfogliatella*, chocolate rum balls rolled in chocolate jimmies, and the famous "S" cookies, dipped in honey or filled with almond paste. Some of these recipes are in this book, but some have been lost over the years.

The singer has everything within him. The notes come out from his very life. They are not materials gathered from outside. ~Rabindranath Tagore

Antipasti ~ Appetizers

I'LL BET YOU think *antipasti* means "after the pasta." It really means, "before the meal." It's served like hors d'oeuvres. You can be as creative as you like with this course. My favorite antipasti dishes are the ones I have in this chapter. You can almost make a full meal out of this course. By including a nice assortment of things like mozzarella cheese balls, roasted eggplant, roasted peppers, breaded and fried zucchini, and marinated mushrooms, you can satisfy the most discerning taste buds and stimulate the palate for the feast to follow. You can combine a little of all these recipes to make a great presentation at a party. Set it in the middle of the table, or have it ready to snack on while you're watching all three of the *Godfather* movies back to back. It's really an offer your guests can't refuse.

Crostini with Gorgonzola, Roasted Peppers, and Balsamic Glaze
Serves 8. Prep time: 30 minutes.

2 red sweet peppers, roasted
2 yellow bell peppers, roasted
½ cup extra virgin olive oil
6 garlic cloves, peeled and divided
10 basil leaves, thinly sliced
3 ounces crumbled Gorgonzola cheese
1 loaf crispy Italian bread, cut into ¼" slices
Sea salt & black pepper
8 tablespoons Balsamic Glaze (recipe next page)

Preheat oven to 450°.

Cut peppers lengthwise and remove seeds. Place on a cookie sheet or baking pan and brush with olive oil. Roast until blackened, about 45 minutes. Place peppers in a bowl, cover with plastic wrap, and let cool.

Remove skin from peppers and cut into ½" slices. Place in a medium bowl. Smash 4 garlic cloves and add to the bowl with the olive oil and basil. Season with salt and pepper. Cover and marinate the peppers in the refrigerator about four hours.

When ready to make the crostini, preheat the oven to 375°. Place bread slices on a baking sheet; drizzle with olive oil and toast until golden brown, about 8 minutes. Transfer to a plate and let cool.

Cut remaining two garlic cloves half and rub cut sides on bread slices. Brush with olive oil. Spread cheese on the crostini and arrange bell pepper mixture over the cheese. Drizzle each with 1 teaspoon of Balsamic Glaze.

Balsamic Glaze
Makes ½ cup

2 cups good balsamic vinegar
1½ teaspoons light honey or brown sugar
1 bay leaf

In a medium saucepan, combine vinegar, honey or brown sugar, and bay leaf. Simmer on low-medium for about 20 minutes, until reduced to ½ cup. Let cool. It will thicken as it cools. Taste and add more sweetener if desired. Remove bay leaf.

This glaze can be stored in a container in the refrigerator for up to 6 months. You can put it in a plastic squeeze bottle to use easily when you need it. Bring to room temperature before using.

Fresh Peaches with Prosciutto & Basil
Serves 24. Prep time: 20 minutes.

3 medium peaches, each cut into 8 wedges
¼ pound prosciutto, sliced thin
¼ teaspoon sugar
½ teaspoon sherry vinegar
¼ teaspoon cardamom

Toss peaches, sugar, vinegar, and cardamom together in a bowl. Let meld for about 10 minutes. Cut prosciutto slices in half lengthwise; wrap each piece around a wedge of peach. Top with a basil leaf and secure with a small toothpick.

Crostini with Caramelized Onions, Roasted Eggplant, and Cracked Green Olives
Serves 8. Prep time: 30 minutes.

1 long loaf of Italian bread
1 large, sweet Spanish onion, cut into ¼" rounds
1 small eggplant, cut into bite-sized pieces
½ cup Italian cracked green olives
Extra virgin olive oil
Salt and freshly ground black pepper

Cut the bread into ¼" slices. Brush with olive oil and toast in oven until golden. In a sauté pan, cook the onions until caramelized and golden brown. Cook the eggplant until soft in the olive oil. Add the chopped olives. Combine all together in a bowl. Top each piece of the bread with the mixture and serve.

For larger servings of onions, place on a baking sheet and brush both sides of the onion with extra virgin olive oil. Caramelize in a 350° oven for about 30 minutes or until brown.

For larger groups, place mixture in a food processor, pulse to semi-soft consistency, and spoon into a piping bag to pipe onto the bread.

Jumbo Calzone Slices with Spinach, Ricotta, and Marinara Sauce Dip
Serves 8-12. Prep time: 60 minutes.

2 pizza doughs, 1 pound each
½ cup ricotta cheese
½ cup cremini mushrooms
4 ounces shredded mozzarella
12 ounces frozen spinach, defrosted and drained well
2 teaspoons ground nutmeg
Salt and black pepper to taste
1½ cups marinara sauce

Preheat oven to 500°.

On a flat surface or wooden floured board, roll out pizza dough. Shape to about a 12" round. Brush with olive oil.

In a sauté pan, cook mushrooms until soft. Set aside.

Drain spinach well so there is no water left and it becomes dry. Mix in grated nutmeg and combine well.

In a bowl, place the ricotta and mix well until smooth. Add the mushrooms, spinach, and salt and pepper to taste.

Place some of the ricotta filling on the pizza dough close to one end, as evenly as possible, without overloading the shell. Fold over the other half of the dough until it resembles a half-moon shape. Pinch the ends with a fork until it is closed.

Brush the outside with olive oil and place on the center of an oiled baking pan. Place in preheated oven for 25 to 30 minutes, or until the calzone is golden brown. Let cool. Cut into 4" to 6" long slices. Dust with parmesan cheese.

Serve with a side of marinara sauce for dipping.

Grilled Pizza
Serves 8. Prep time: 60 minutes.

1 recipe Andy's Pizza Sauce (recipe follows)
¼ ounce (1 package) active dry yeast (instant can be used)
1 teaspoon sugar
1 cup warm water (105° - 115°)
3 cups all-purpose flour, plus more if needed (Italian OO flour is the best if available;
     bread flour can also be used)
1 teaspoon sea salt
3 tablespoons olive oil, plus more if needed
Toppings as desired

In a small bowl or measuring cup, stir yeast and sugar into warm water and let sit for 5 minutes until foamy. (If using instant yeast, skip this step and add the dry yeast to the flour.) Place flour and salt in the work bowl of a food processor. Turn on and slowly pour the yeast mixture through the feed tube and let the dough come together. Add the oil though the feed tube and process the dough until it clings to the side of the bowl but is still moist. If it's too sticky, add more flour; if too dry, add more water. Process until kneaded, about 40 seconds. The dough should be supple and elastic when you stretch it with your hands.

Transfer the dough to a large plastic food bag that has been sprayed with oil; alternatively, you can cover the dough with a little flour to prevent it from sticking. Squeeze all the air out of the bag and seal the top, leaving room inside for the dough to expand. Place the bag in a bowl and let it rise in a warm spot until doubled, about 1 hour. Punch the dough down. The dough can be used now or refrigerated for up to 5 days.

Divide the dough into 4 equal portions of about 6 ounces each. Roll each piece on a cutting board with some flour to make about an 8" circle or rectangle crust. Stack the crusts between oiled sheets of waxed paper. It can be rolled in advance and refrigerated several hours or frozen.

When ready to use, brush a crust with olive oil on one side and place on a grill heated to 500°. Cover grill with lid and grill until marks show. Keep rotating the dough until golden and crisp. Turn the dough over and top with desired toppings: the cheeses first, then the sauce, then other toppings.

Suggested toppings:
½ cup extra-virgin olive oil
2 teaspoons minced garlic
2 cups fontina cheese
⅔ cup grated Pecorino Romano cheese
1⅓ cups canned tomatoes, in heavy purée or chopped
Andy's Pizza Sauce (recipe below)
½ cup thinly-sliced basil leaves
2 cups fresh thyme

Cook until sauce and cheese bubble. Cut and serve.

If using the oven, heat to 450°. Place on a pizza stone on the bottom rack. Use a floured pizza peal or paddle to slide in and out of oven.

Andy's Pizza Sauce
Yields about 1 quart. Prep time: 10 minutes.

3 to 6 pounds fresh Roma Italian tomatoes
2 - 3 cloves garlic
8 fresh basil leaves
Kosher salt
Olive oil

Halve tomatoes and brush with olive oil. Roast in a 400° oven. Drain, remove seeds, and place in blender with remaining ingredients. Blend well. Taste and adjust seasoning if needed. Spoon ¼ cup of sauce onto each pizza. Do not over-sauce.

Grilled Shrimp and Polenta Wedges with Feta Cheese and Roasted Red Pepper Sauce
Serves 6. Prep time: 30 minutes.

12 medium to large shrimp (16-20 count per pound), de-veined with tails on
1 bay leaf
½ cup hard feta or Gorgonzola cheese, broken
1 cup yellow polenta
½ cup parmesan cheese
Mint leaves
2 to 3 medium red bell peppers
¾ cup chicken stock
Extra virgin olive oil

In a saucepan, bring four to five cups of salted water to a rolling boil. Add bay leaf. Reduce the heat and slowly add the polenta, stirring all the time with a whisk, until polenta sticks to the sides of the pan.

Add the parmesan cheese and stir until smooth. Pour out onto a ¼" sheet pan and let cool on the counter or in the refrigerator.

For the roasted red pepper sauce, heat the oven to 400°. Halve and de-seed the peppers, and place on a baking sheet. Drizzle extra virgin olive oil over the peppers. Sprinkle with salt and pepper and place in the heated oven for 45 minutes, or until peppers are soft and skin is brown. Remove from oven, let cool, and place in a blender or food processor. Add the chicken stock and pulse until blended. Salt and pepper to taste. Place in a squeeze bottle and set aside.

Heat the grill. In a bowl with olive oil, add garlic, salt, and pepper. Add shrimp and coat on both sides. Put the shrimp on the hot grill and cook for a few minutes on both sides until done.

Cut polenta into 2" triangles and coat with olive oil. Place on the grill and cook on both sides until grill marks appear. Place shrimp and polenta on a dish and add the crumbled feta cheese. Garnish with fresh mint leaves and swirls of roasted red pepper sauce on the top and around the dish to serve.

Sicilian Caponata on Grilled Crostini
Serves 6. Prep time: 40 minutes.

1 medium Italian eggplant, cut into small cubes
½ sweet onion, chopped
1 sweet red bell pepper, chopped
½ cup Kalamata olives
½ cup cracked green olives
½ cup golden raisins
¼ cup red wine vinegar
½ teaspoon sugar
½ cup capers
½ teaspoon red pepper flakes
1 cup crushed or diced plum tomatoes
3 basil leaves
½ cup olive oil
Salt and black pepper to taste
1 loaf Italian bread, cut into ¼" slices, brushed with olive oil and grilled or toasted until golden brown.

Cut and cube eggplant and place into a colander. Add ¼ cup of salt. Put a weight or plate on the top to help drain the bitterness out. After 1 hour, drain and rinse well. Pat dry.

In a deep pan or pot, add onions, peppers, and celery. Season with salt and pepper. Heat on medium-high and cook until soft and translucent. Add remaining ingredients (except bread) and cook for 20 more minutes over low heat. Taste for seasoning and adjust as desired.

Serve on top of the grilled bread. Pour a glass of good red table wine and enjoy!

Stuffed Portabella Mushrooms
Serves 4. Prep time: 30 minutes.

4 large portobello mushrooms, washed and gills cleaned
4 thin slices Italian prosciutto ham
4 tablespoons sultana raisins
4 tablespoons extra virgin olive oil
½ small onion, chopped and peeled
2 thinly sliced and peeled garlic cloves
2 bunches washed and trimmed spinach, about 2 to 3 pounds
3 tablespoons toasted pine nuts
1 tablespoon fresh lemon juice
8 thin strips lemon zest
Salt and black pepper to taste

Soak the raisins in a bowl of cold water for 10 minutes; drain and set aside.

Heat olive oil in a large skillet over medium heat. Add chopped onion and garlic cloves; cook until soft, about 4-5 minutes. Add the spinach and cook, stirring, 1 minute. Cover and cook until wilted, 2-3 minutes. Add toasted pine nuts, fresh lemon juice, lemon zest, and raisins. Season to taste.

Sauté mushrooms in olive oil on both sides until soft. Stuff with spinach mixture, put a thin slice of Italian prosciutto over the top, and shave some imported pecorino or parmesan cheese over it all. Place under the broiler for one or two minutes. Mushrooms can also be grilled first before stuffing.

Serve with lemon wedges.

Bruschetta with Yellow and Red Tomatoes and Buffalo Mozzarella
Serves 20. Prep time: 30 minutes.

1 thin, long loaf of Italian bread, or one ciabatta bread
1 medium yellow tomato, diced
1 medium red tomato, diced
6 ounces fresh buffalo mozzarella, diced
½ cup fresh basil chiffonade
3 cloves of garlic, diced
¼ cup extra virgin olive oil
Balsamic vinegar
Kosher salt and freshly ground black pepper

Cut bread into ¼" slices, dip in olive oil, and toast under the broiler until golden brown.

Combine remaining ingredients in a medium bowl and mix well. Let sit for 10 minutes or overnight in the refrigerator.

Spoon a little onto each slice of bread and serve with a drizzle of balsamic vinegar on the top.

Prosciutto di Parma-Wrapped Garlic Spinach Balls
Makes 60 balls. Prep time: 40 minutes.

2 packages frozen, chopped spinach, defrosted and drained well
2 cups seasoned Italian bread crumbs, plus 1 cup extra
1 pound imported Prosciutto di Parma
6 eggs, beaten
2 medium yellow onions, chopped fine
½ cup Italian parsley, chopped fine
¾ cup melted butter, brought to room temperature
½ cup freshly-grated parmesan cheese
4 garlic cloves, minced
Freshly ground black pepper
Kosher salt to taste
Red pepper flakes to taste

Preheat oven to 350°. Line a baking sheet with parchment paper.

In a food processor, chop Italian parsley, onions, and garlic.

In a large bowl, mix the eggs, melted butter, spinach, salt and pepper, red pepper flakes, onions, parsley and garlic. Add the bread crumbs and mix by hand until it all comes together. Add more bread crumbs if needed to desired consistency.

Put mix into the refrigerator for about 15 minutes, until mix is firm. Using teaspoon-size portions, roll into small balls in your hand. Place balls on baking sheet and bake for 15 minutes, or until slightly browned on both sides.

Wrap with Prosciutto di Parma and serve.

Assorted Italian and Greek Olives with Prosciutto-Wrapped Grissini
Serve 6. Prep time: 20 minutes.

¼ cup Kalamata olives
¼ cup Gaeta olives
¼ cracked green olives
¼ cup Castelvetrano olives
¼ cup Nyon olives
¼ cup Niçoise olives
1 box (4 ounces) grissini gticks
12 thin slices imported Italian prosciutto

Combine all of the olives above in a medium sized bowl. Toss well.

Serve on a small plate or in a small bowl topped with two prosciutto-wrapped grissini sticks.

Kalamata Olive Tapenade
Serves 8. Prep time: 20 minutes.

3 cloves garlic, peeled
1 cup pitted Kalamata Olives
2 tablespoons capers
3 tablespoons chopped Italian parsley
2 tablespoons lemon juice
2 tablespoons olive oil
Salt and pepper to taste

Place garlic cloves into a blender or food processor and pulse to mince. Add the olives, capers, parsley, lemon juice, and olive oil. Blend until all is finely chopped. Season with salt and pepper.

Deep-Fried Ravioli with Marinara Sauce
Serves 8. Prep time: 30 minutes.

24 fresh or frozen cheese ravioli
2 cups Italian bread crumbs
1 cup buttermilk
¼ cup freshly-grated parmesan cheese
1 jar (16 ounces) marinara sauce

Heat olive oil in a deep skillet or cast-iron pan to 325°.

While oil is heating, put buttermilk and bread crumbs each in a separate shallow bowl. Dip each raviolo in buttermilk and shake off the excess; then dip into the breadcrumbs, making sure to coat on both sides. Place on a sheet pan. Prepare all ravioli the same way.

When the oil is 325°, fry a few ravioli at a time, making sure to fry both sides until golden brown, about 2 minutes. Using a slotted spoon, transfer each raviolo to a baking sheet lined with paper towels and let drain. Sprinkle with sea salt and parmesan cheese. Place several ravioli on a plate, top with marinara sauce, and present with a sprig or two of fresh or crispy basil.

Fresh Wild Salmon Cakes with Garlic Aioli in Grilled Radicchio Leaves
Serves 4. Prep time: 30 minutes.

1¼ pounds fresh wild salmon, coarsely chopped
¼ cup minced sweet onion
2 tablespoons minced red bell pepper
2 tablespoons minced celery
2 tablespoons capers
¼ cup mayonnaise
¼ cup Italian or Panko bread crumbs
1 teaspoon Dijon mustard
1 teaspoon minced garlic
Pinch of cayenne pepper
¼ cup extra virgin olive oil for frying
Sea salt and freshly ground black pepper to taste
Garlic aioli or tartar sauce
4 to 6 outside leafs of round radicchio lettuce, lightly grilled

Heat olive oil in skillet over medium heat. Add red bell pepper, onion, and celery and season with salt. Simmer until onion is translucent, about 5 minutes. Add capers and stir until fragrant. Remove from heat and cool to room temperature.

In a medium bowl, stir chopped salmon, onion mixture, mayonnaise, minced garlic, mustard, cayenne, sea salt, and pepper. Mix well. Cover with plastic wrap and refrigerate until firmed and chilled, about 1 to 2 hours.

Form salmon mixture into 4 to 6 medium-sized patties. Sprinkle each patty with a coating of Panko or bread crumbs. Heat olive oil in skillet over medium heat. Pan-fry patties in medium heat until golden and cooked through, about 2 to 3 minutes on each side.

Serve in grilled radicchio leaves with a drizzle of garlic aioli or tartar sauce.

Singing provides a true sense of lightheartedness. If I sing when I am alone,
I feel wonderful, it's freedom! ~Andrea Bocelli

Salads

I'VE ALWAYS LIKED sunshine, and the color green. The grass around our house was always rich with color, especially in the summer. It was a real blessing to see summer roll around and watch our garden grow. My Grandfather Lo Russo seemed to practice magic when he brought the garden to life year after year. The best red tomatoes and the different varieties of lettuce, cucumbers, carrots, and beets would come right from the yard onto the dinner table.

In Italy, like much of Europe, salads are eaten at the end of the meal, particularly after pasta. It helps digestion. Some people enjoy salad before the meal, or, like me, during. Whatever your choice, you should see greens on your table daily. "*Non giorno sensa verdura, non giorno sensa sole* (A day without greens is like a day without sunshine)." With salads, remember that the key word is "fresh."

The Greener the Green, the Better

(Based on a 3.5 oz. serving)

Green	Vitamin A	Vitamin C	Calcium
	(Int'l. Units)	*(Mg)*	*(Mg)*
Arugula	7,400	91	6830935
Spinach	6,715	28	999
Watercress	4,700	43	120
Chicory	4,000	24	100
Romaine	2,600	24	36
Red Leaf	1,900	18	68
Boston or Bibb	970	8	35
Iceberg	330	4	19

Burrata Cheese and Heirloom Tomatos

Serves 6. Prep time: 20 minutes.

6 burrata cheese balls, 2.2 ounces each
5 large, heirloom, plum tomatoes, about 3½ pounds
Sea salt and freshly ground black pepper
½ cup torn fresh basil leaves
¼ cup extra virgin olive oil
Balsamic vinegar to drizzle
1 cup baby organic arugula

Cut tomatoes into wedges and place in a medium bowl. Sprinkle with salt and black pepper and toss well. Drizzle some balsamic over wedges and mix again. Add torn basil leaves.

On salad plates, place arugula in the center. Put one burrata ball on the top of the arugula. Spread the tomatoes around the burrata on the plate. Drizzle with more balsamic vinegar. Add more salt and pepper if desired.

Marinated Vegetables and Olive Salad
Serves 12. Prep time: 30 minutes.

1 large (about 2½ pounds) cauliflower
1 pound carrots, peeled
½ cup extra virgin olive oil
¼ cup red wine vinegar
⅓ cup flat-leaf parsley, chopped
1 teaspoon sugar
¾ teaspoon kosher salt
½ teaspoon dry mustard
¼ teaspoon ground black pepper
½ teaspoon red pepper flakes
1 cup brine-cured green and ripe olives
Fresh flat-leaf parsley sprigs (optional)

Trim cauliflower and separate or cut small flowerets. Cut carrots into matchsticks.

In a 5-quart saucepan, heat 2" of water to boiling over high heat. Add carrots and bring back to a boil. Add cauliflower to water with carrots. Cook vegetables just until tender-crisp. Drain and rinse with cold water, then set aside in a large bowl or food storage container.

In a jar with a tight-fitting lid, combine oil, vinegar, chopped parsley, sugar, salt, dry mustard, and peppers until well mixed. Pour over vegetables, toss, and cover. Refrigerate 2 hours or overnight, stirring occasionally.

Just before serving, add olives to vegetables and toss until well mixed. Spoon into serving bowl. Garnish with parsley sprigs, if desired.

Sweet Fennel and Orange Salad with Toasted Walnuts in a Honey-Sherry Vinaigrette
Serves 6-8. Prep time: 15 minutes.

2 medium fennel bulbs, shredded
4 medium-sized sweet oranges, cut into rounds
2 cups fresh arugula or mixed greens
2 small shallots, minced
2 spoons light honey
¼ cup sherry vinegar
1 lemon, juiced
1 orange, juiced
¼ cup extra virgin olive oil
Salt and freshly ground black pepper
¼ cup toasted walnut bits

Wash and trim salad. Peel and cut oranges into rounds or sections, removing seeds.

Whisk, honey, lemon juice, shallots, salt, orange juice, and sherry vinegar together. Add olive oil and black pepper. Whisk until blended.

Place salad on plate and top with fennel and orange slices. Spoon dressing over the salad and top with toasted chopped walnuts.

Panzanella Salad Tuscan Style
Serves 6. Prep time: 30 minutes.

¾ pound ciabatta or sourdough bread, cut into 1½" cubes, to make 6 cups
2 ½ pounds pear or cherry tomatoes cut into bite-sized pieces
1 small shallot, minced
3 cloves of garlic, minced
½ teaspoon Dijon mustard
2 tablespoons red or white wine vinegar
1 cup fresh basil leaves, roughly chopped
Sea salt & freshly ground black pepper to taste
¼ cup extra virgin olive oil

In a colander, place cut tomatoes and season with the sea salt. Toss well. Drain for about 15 minutes, reserving juice.

Preheat the oven to 350°.

In a medium bowl toss the cut bread in with the olive oil and mix until well coated. Place on baking sheet and bake until firm, about 15 minutes. Let cool.

Place tomatoes with juice from colander in a medium bowl; add shallot, garlic, mustard, and vinegar. Mix with some olive oil and season with salt and pepper to taste. Add the bread cubes and mix well. Let rest 30 minutes, or until the bread cubes have absorbed all the dressing.

Add some fresh basil leaves. Toss again. Serve on salad plates or bowls.

Grilled Shrimp, Fennel, and Radicchio with Balsamic Syrup
Serves 4. Prep time: 20 minutes.

12 medium shrimp, shells and veins removed, tails left on (small Bay shrimp can also be used)
1 medium fennel bulb, cut lengthwise into bite-sized pieces
4 large oranges, top cut off and center taken out (optional)
1 cup Mandarin orange slices (optional)
4 medium to large radicchio leaves cut into small strips (large leaves can be used as container for salad)
Extra virgin olive oil
Freshly ground black pepper
Kosher salt

Heat the grill to 375°-400°.

Marinate the shrimp in a medium bowl with olive oil and some salt for a few minutes.

Cut the fennel and the radicchio into strips and place in another bowl with olive oil and seasoning.

Grill the shrimp, Mandarin orange slices, radicchio, and fennel on both sides.

Stuff the oranges with the fennel and the radicchio and some of the Mandarin orange wedges. If using large shrimp, hang a few off of the sides of the oranges. Drizzle with a little olive oil and serve.

Balsamic Syrup
In a saucepan, place one cup of balsamic vinegar and ¼ cup sugar. Over medium to low heat, reduce to about ½ cup until it thickens and turns into a syrup-like consistency. Put into a squeeze bottle.

Option 2
Place all the ingredients in a grilled radicchio leaf. Drizzle with olive oil, salt, and black pepper. Pour some orange juice over it. Small bay shrimp can be used for this, or sautéed medium-to-large shrimp.

Mozzarella alla Caprese Tower with Grilled Eggplant Slices
Serves 4. Prep Time 30 minutes.

4 balls of fresh buffalo mozzarella or 4 balls of fresh soft mozzarella
4 medium, fresh, ripe tomatoes, red or yellow
2 medium Italian eggplant, cut into even ¼" rounds, skin on
1 bunch fresh basil
Balsamic vinegar
Extra virgin olive oil
Salt and freshly ground black pepper

Heat grill.

Leaving the skin on, cut the eggplant into rounds, as evenly as you can. Cut 4 or 5 rounds for each tower. Brush with olive oil and grill on both sides until done. There should be grill marks on each one. Season with salt and pepper.

Cut thin, round slices of the mozzarella cheese so that you have about 4 or 5 slices for each tower.

Cut the tomatoes into round slices, 4 or 5 slices per tower.

Layer the eggplant, mozzarella, tomatoes, and basil until you have used at least 4 of each ingredient. Drizzle with olive oil.

Roasted Sweet Red Peppers, Balsamic-Marinated Porcini Mushrooms, and Caramelized Pecans on a Bed of Baby Greens
Serves 4-6. Prep time: 30 minutes.

4 sweet red bell peppers
1 cup Porcini or Shiitake mushrooms
2 cloves garlic
2 tablespoons lemon juice
½ cup pecans
½ stick butter
¼ cup flour
¼ cup honey
½ cup extra virgin olive oil
½ cup balsamic vinegar
1 bag baby greens
¼ cup pomegranate seeds (in season)

Preheat oven to 400°.

Cut peppers in rounds and remove seeds. Oil them, place on a baking sheet, and roast until done, about 40 minutes.

Chop mushrooms and sauté in olive oil for about 3 minutes. Place mushrooms and roasted peppers in a bowl with balsamic vinegar, salt, and black pepper. Let marinate for about 5 minutes. Add some chopped garlic to this.

In a fry pan, melt butter and add pecans. Sprinkle on the flour and drizzle the honey over pecans to coat. Toast until pecans are soft and caramelized.

Add peppers and mushrooms to the pan and cook for 1 minute. Pour over baby greens. Drizzle some balsamic and lemon juice over the salad. Garnish with pomegranate seeds.

Bocconcini Caprese Salad

Serves 6. Prep time: 20 minutes.

1 cup bocconcini (bite-sized) mozzarella balls, drained and halved
1 pint multi-colored, heirloom cherry tomatoes, halved
1 lemon, juiced
1 garlic clove, grated or minced
⅓ cup extra virgin olive oil
1 cup basil leaves (about 20), plus extra for garnish
¼ cup fresh mint leaves
Kosher salt and freshly ground black pepper

In a blender or food processor, process basil, lemon juice, garlic, in extra virgin olive oil to form a smooth dressing.

In a medium bowl, combine tomatoes, cheese, and dressing, and season with kosher salt and black pepper. Toss in extra basil leave with a few leaves of fresh mint.

Escarole with Walnuts, Anchovies, and Parmesan

Serves 4. Prep time: 20 minutes.

2 heads escarole
½ cup celery heart, sliced thinly
¼ pound parmesan, sliced thinly
⅓ cup walnuts, broken
1 can anchovy fillets, finely chopped
¾ cup olive oil
¼ cup lemon juice or red wine vinegar
2 pounds parsley, minced
Ground pepper

Wash the escarole and combine with celery, parmesan, and walnuts. Whisk together anchovies, olive oil, lemon juice or red wine vinegar, parsley, and pepper.
Pour over salad and toss.

Belgium Endive with Goat Cheese and Toasted Walnuts
Serves 6. Prep time: 20 minutes.

6 large Belgian endive leaves
½ cup celery hearts, sliced thin
½ cup walnuts, halved or broken
4 to 5 ounces imported goat cheese
Lemon Anchovy Dressing (recipe below)

Wash the Belgian endive well. Combine the celery hearts, walnuts, and endive in a bowl.

Lemon Anchovy Dressing

1 can anchovy fillets, washed well and finely chopped
¾ cup extra virgin olive oil
¼ cup fresh lemon juice
Black pepper to taste

In another bowl, whisk the olive oil, lemon juice, and anchovies. Season with black pepper to taste.

Pour dressing over salad. Divide the mix equally on 6 plates and sprinkle liberally with goat cheese.

Italian Potato Salad with Sun-Dried Tomatoes
Serves 6-8. Prep time: 30 Minutes.

4 pounds small red or Yukon Gold potatoes, cut in half
4 celery stalks, finely chopped
4 ounces sun-dried tomatoes packed in olive oil, drained
¼ cup extra virgin olive oil
1 teaspoon kosher salt
1 teaspoon freshly ground black pepper
¼ teaspoon red pepper flakes (optional)
¼ cup Italian flat-leaf parsley, chopped
6 slices applewood-smoked bacon, crumbled or ¼ cup bacon bits
2 teaspoons caraway seeds
1 medium red onion, finely chopped
3 tablespoons red wine vinegar, plus more if needed
2 teaspoons Dijon mustard

Place potatoes in a large saucepan. Cover with water to about 1" over the top. Over medium-high heat, bring pot to a boil. Reduce heat and simmer until cooked through but not too soft, about 15 minutes. Drain and let cool.

In a small bowl, whisk the olive oil, mustard, vinegar, salt, pepper, and red pepper flakes. Mix in remaining ingredients and pour the dressing over the potatoes. Toss gently. Adjust seasoning to taste.

Keep cold in the refrigerator for up to 1 day.

I don't know what happens to me on stage, something else seems to take over.
~Maria Callas

Soups

SOMEONE ONCE SAID, "You can always tell if the main course is going to be a hit if the soup is good." In most cases, it's the truth. The next time you go out for dinner and the soup is not quite what you expected, especially if it's cold, you had better ask for the check and have the main course elsewhere.

I always enjoy my soup hot—not boiling, but palatable. This warms me up for the meal to follow. It says that the chef is concerned enough to pay attention to what is being served right from the start. It's like foreplay, preparing the family and the guests for what is to follow.

In this section, I give you some of my favorite soup recipes. There are many more that complement the Italian meal, but these are the most loved and enjoyed by everyone. The Pasta Fagiole is a classic, real down-home, on-the-farm, Italian-style cooking at its best. The Minestrone is one of the soups that put a little bit of Italian in every household.

Remember: always have some fresh, grated parmesan cheese and some Italian bread on the table. They add so much to the enjoyment of the soup. Enjoy!

Italian Chicken Soup with Orzo Pasta, Parmesan Cheese, and Fresh Lemon
Serves 6. Prep time: 40 minutes.

10 ounces boneless, skinless free-range chicken breast
6 cups low-sodium chicken broth
½ cup orzo pasta
1 cup water
2 medium carrots, diced
⅔ cups celery
⅔ cups sweet onion, chopped
2 tablespoons rosemary
2 tablespoons thyme
Sea salt and freshly ground black pepper
¼ cup lemon juice
¼ cup baby arugula leaves or spinach leaves
½ cup freshly grated parmesan or pecorino cheese

In a large soup pot, sauté the onions, carrots, and celery until translucent. Add the water and chicken stock. Place the boneless chicken breasts in and bring to a boil. Lower the heat and cook for about 1½ hours, or until the chicken is soft and cooked through.

Remove the chicken and break it apart with a knife into thin pieces.

Cook pasta in another pot of boiling, salted water. Drain well. Add the chicken back to the soup pot, then add the herbs and the pasta. Add the arugula or spinach leaves and the lemon juice. Stir for about 1 minute.

Separate into bowls and grate some fresh parmesan or pecorino cheese on the top.

Pasta Fagioli with Roasted Garlic Crostini
Serves 8. Prep time: 40 minutes.

32 ounces white cannellini beans (or two 15 ounce cans), soaked overnight (Red kidney beans, garbanzo beans, or cranberry beans may also be used.)
8 cups chicken stock
1 large onion, diced
¼ cup extra virgin olive oil
1 can (14 ounces) stewed tomatoes, drained; or, 1 pound Roma tomatoes, skins removed, de-seeded, and chopped
3 cloves garlic, diced
1 pound ditalini, small shells, or elbow pasta
¼ to ½ pound Pancetta ham, cut into small pieces
¼ cup freshly-grated parmesan cheese
Freshly ground black pepper to taste
Kosher salt
1 loaf Italian bread
1 bulb fresh garlic

In a 2 quart sauté pan or sauce pot, heat olive oil, garlic, and onion. Cook over low heat. Add pancetta ham. Cook a few minutes, then add tomatoes and simmer for a few more minutes.

In another pot, add beans and enough water to cover. Cook until soft but not mushy. If you use canned beans, add to 6 cups chicken stock and bring to a low simmer.

Cook the pasta in another pot until *al dente*, then add to stock.

Pour into bowls and grate parmesan cheese over the top. Sprinkle with black pepper.

Cut bread into ¼" slices; dip in olive oil and toast in 350° oven until golden brown. Cut off top of garlic bulb and drizzle with olive oil. Wrap in foil and bake in 400° oven for about 45 minutes or until the cloves are soft. Take out garlic and squeeze a clove on each piece of bread. Serve with soup.

Traditional Italian Wedding Soup
Serves 8. Prep time: 40 minutes.

For the Meatballs:
1 small onion, grated
⅓ cup chopped fresh Italian flat-leaf parsley
1 large egg
2 teaspoons minced garlic
1 teaspoon salt
1 slice fresh white bread, crust removed, torn into small pieces
½ cup freshly-grated parmesan cheese
8 ounces ground beef
8 ounces ground pork
Freshly ground black pepper

To make the meatballs, mix the first 6 ingredients in a large bowl and blend. Stir in the cheese, beef, and pork. Season with salt and pepper. Using 1½ teaspoons for each, shape into 1" diameter balls. Brown them in a skillet until cooked on both sides.

For the Soup:
12 cups low-sodium chicken broth (my preference is to use 3 cartons, 32 ounces each, organic chicken broth)
1 pound curly endive or escarole, coarsely chopped
1 pound orzo pasta
2 large eggs
4 tablespoons freshly-grated parmesan cheese, plus extra for garnish
Kosher salt and freshly ground black pepper

For the soup, bring the chicken broth to a boil in a large pot over medium-high heat. Add the meatballs and curly endive or escarole, and simmer until the meatballs are cooked through and the curly endive is tender, about 8 minutes.

Whisk the eggs and cheese in a medium bowl to blend. Stir the soup in a circular motion. Gradually drizzle the egg mixture into the moving broth, stirring gently with a fork to form thin strands of egg, about 1 minute. Season the soup with salt and pepper.

Cook orzo pasta in separate pot until *al dente*. Add some to each bowl. Ladle soup over pasta, stir, and serve. Sprinkle parmesan cheese over the top.

Chicken Tortellini Soup with Crunchy Pancetta Bits
Serves 6. Prep time: 30 minutes.

8 ounces chicken tortellini
1 small onion, diced
1 medium carrot, diced
1 red bell pepper, diced
2 Italian hot chili peppers or Thai chili peppers (optional)
½ pound pancetta, chopped into small cubes
1 can (15 ounces) diced San Marzano tomatoes, or regular tomatoes
2 cloves garlic, diced
6 cups low-sodium chicken broth
Freshly grated parmesan cheese
1 cup fresh baby spinach, washed and stems removed
Sea salt and freshly ground black pepper to taste

In a large soup pot, sauté the pancetta until crispy.

Remove from pot, then sauté the carrots, onion, celery, and garlic in the pancetta fat. Add some olive oil if needed.

Add the chicken stock and bring to a boil. Add the tortellini pasta and bring back to a slow boil. Add the peppers and simmer until pasta is al dente.

Add the baby spinach and the crunchy pancetta bits and cook on low heat for 2 minutes. Add salt and black pepper to taste.

Serve in soup bowl topped with the freshly grated cheese.

Stracciatella Soup with Roasted Garlic Crostini Floats
Serves 4. Prep time: 30 minutes.

1 loaf Italian or French crusty baguette
4 cloves roasted garlic
6 cups chicken broth
2 large eggs
2 tablespoons freshly grated parmesan cheese
2 tablespoons Italian flat-leaf parsley, chopped
2 tablespoons fresh basil leaves
1 cup lightly packed fresh spinach

Cut bread into ¼" slices and place on baking sheet. Drizzle with olive oil and place in 350° oven. Roast until golden brown. You can also put the garlic cloves on this pan or wrap the cloves up in aluminum foil and roast until soft, about 20 minutes.

Bring chicken broth to boil in a large saucepan over medium-high heat.

In a bowl, whisk the eggs, cheese, parsley, and basil to blend. Reduce the heat to medium-low. Stir the broth in a circular motion. Gradually drizzle the egg mixture into the moving broth, stirring gently with a fork to form thin strands of egg, and cook for 1 minute. Stir in the spinach, then season with salt and pepper to taste.

Spread the roasted garlic on slices of crostini. Ladle soup into bowls and float a crostini slice on top.

Baccala –**Cod Fish Soup**

Serves 6. Prep time: 60 minutes.

1½ pounds baccalà (salt cod)
2 small onions, sliced thin
3 stalks celery, diced
1 bay leaf
2 stems parsley, diced
28 ounces San Marzano tomatoes, crushed
3 medium Yukon gold potatoes, cubed
4 cups water
½ teaspoon thyme
Sea salt and black pepper to taste

Soak the baccalà (dried, salted cod) in a deep pan of water in the refrigerator for two days. Change the water each day.

Cut the cod into 4" cubes and set aside.

In a 4-quart soup pot over medium heat, add the olive oil, onion, and garlic; cook until brown. Add celery, bay leaf, thyme, and parley, and continue cooking for two minutes. Add the 4 cups of water or vegetable broth, the tomatoes, and the potatoes and cook for 10 more minutes.

Add the baccalà, cover, and cook for about 20 minutes on low heat, until the fish and vegetables are soft. Serve in soup bowls.

The only thing better than singing is more singing. ~Ella Fitzgerald

Sandwiches

The Art of the Sandwich

IT IS SAID the sandwich got its name from John Montagu, 4th Earl of Sandwich, an 18th-century English aristocrat who was very hungry after playing for a long time at the gaming table without anything to eat. He asked his valet to bring him two slices of bread with some beef between them, and thus the sandwich was born. We do not know if this is the absolute truth, but today it is said that each person consumes over 200 sandwiches per year.

My father, Andy (for whom I was named), was very creative in the kitchen. Some of my fondest memories of him are when he and I would drive to the Jersey Shore to go fishing.

He would make these sandwiches early in the morning, about 4:00 a.m., just before we loaded up the car. It was a 2-hour drive to catch one of the fishing boats that had been waiting to take us out to catch blue fish or mackerel.

He would take these sandwiches, wrap them up, put them in a brown paper bag, and put them in the cooler along with plenty of beer and orange soda. By the time we got to our destination, the olive oil was oozing from the warm pepper-and-eggs sandwiches and turned the paper bags all dark brown. I think I ate most of these unctuous, tasty treats while he reeled in the big fish. If we were lucky, we would take some fresh fish home for dinner.

Dad's Italian Pepper and Egg Sandwich
Makes 4. Prep time: 30 minutes.

4 soft Italian rolls; or, 1 loaf Italian bread cut into 4 equal pieces
4 medium cubanelle or green bell peppers, washed, seeded, and sliced thin
4 large eggs, beaten with 1 tablespoon milk
2 cloves garlic, finely chopped
1 medium sweet onion, chopped
¼ cup extra virgin olive oil
¼ cup parmesan and pecorino cheese, grated
Crushed red pepper flakes
Sea salt and freshly ground black pepper

In a medium to large sauté pan over low heat, place the extra virgin olive oil, garlic, and onion, and sauté about 1 minute until the onion is translucent. Add the peppers and cook over medium heat for about 3 minutes, or until the peppers are soft. Season with salt and pepper.

Raise the heat to medium-high and add the beaten eggs, making sure to coat all the peppers evenly and being careful not to burn them. Turn down the heat, cover with a plate, and cook for 1 to 2 minutes until eggs are done.

Take each Italian roll, split, and drizzle some olive oil in each, then sprinkle with cheese and red pepper flakes. Place one fourth of egg mixture in each split roll.

If going fishing, wrap with plastic wrap and place into brown paper sandwich bags. Thanks, Dad.

Grilled Beef Ciabatta Sandwiches with Melted Cheese, Beefsteak Tomatoes, Capers, and Olives
Serves 4-8. Prep time: 40 minutes.

2 pounds top round steak, cut very thin for grilling, about ¼ pound per person; or
    2 pounds beef strip steaks, cut ¾" thick, about 2 ounces per person
¼ cup extra virgin olive oil
Kosher salt and freshly ground black pepper
1 large loaf ciabatta bread, sliced lengthwise; or,
    individual ciabatta rolls or Italian bread rolls
1½ cups shredded Fontana cheese or triple cheese (mozzarella, fontina, cheddar) mix; or
    1 cup white cheddar cheese, shredded
½ cup medium onion, chopped
4 garlic cloves, chopped
1 can (14 ounces) of Italian San Marzano peeled tomatoes, drained and chopped; or
    4 to 5 large beefsteak tomatoes, chopped
1 cup Kalamata olives or black olives, pitted and chopped
3 tablespoons capers, minced and drained
½ cup water
1 cup red wine

Trim steaks and cut horizontally in half so they are very thin. Pound steaks between two pieces of plastic wrap until flattened to ½" thickness. Brush with olive oil and season with salt and pepper. You can also marinate the streaks in minced garlic, salt, and olive oil in a plastic bag for a few hours.

In a sauté pan, heat olive oil over medium heat. Add onion and cook 2 to 3 minutes or until softened. Add garlic and cook for 1 more minute. Add tomatoes, olives, capers, and red wine. Bring to a boil, then reduce heat to medium low, cover, and cook 5 minutes. Season with salt and pepper.

Fire up the grill to medium-high heat, 375°. Grill the beef about 3" from the heat for 4 minutes on each side. Cut ciabatta bread lengthwise, keeping one side connected. Brush with olive oil and garlic. Place cut side down on grill, putting something heavy on the top to get those great grill marks. Remove ciabatta from the grill and place grilled beef strips on one side. Pour some sauce over the top and cover with the cheese. Close up the sandwich and place back on the grill for a few minutes until the cheese melts.

Remove to cutting board and slice into 2 to 3" servings.

Turkey Meatball Open-Faced Sandwich with Buffalo Mozzarella & Tomato Basil Sauce
Serves 6. Prep time: 40 minutes.

1 pound dark meat ground turkey
1 medium white onion, minced
1 cup Italian bread crumbs
½ cup parmesan cheese
2 eggs, beaten
¼ cup whole milk, room temperature
1 teaspoon tomato paste
¼ cup basil leaves, chopped
2 garlic cloves, chopped
¼ cup parsley, chopped
8 ounces fresh buffalo mozzarella
16 ounces tomato-basil marinara sauce
1 whole loaf ciabatta bread, cut into ¼" slices
¼ cup extra virgin olive oil
Sea salt and freshly ground black pepper
½ cup basil leaves, for garnish

Heat the oven to 400°.

In a medium bowl, combine bread crumbs, milk, eggs, tomato paste, onion, parsley, salt, and pepper; mix well. Add the ground turkey and mix well with your hands. Form the turkey into medium-sized balls in your hands. Place on a ¼" baking sheet and drizzle with olive oil. Place in the oven for 15 minutes.

In another ¼" baking sheet, place the ciabatta slices and drizzle with olive oil. Place in the oven and cook until golden brown on the top, about 10 minutes.

In a medium sauce pan, heat the tomato-basil marinara sauce. Remove the meatballs from the oven; add them to the sauce and simmer over low heat for 5 to 10 minutes.

Remove both baking pans from the oven. Let cool for a few minutes.

Cut each meatball in half and place three slices on the top of each ciabatta slice. Spoon sauce over each meatball until well coated. Place a thin slice or two of buffalo mozzarella on the top of each meatball. Place back into the oven for 6 to 10 minutes, until the cheese starts to bubble and melt over the sides of the bread.

Remove from oven and let cool. Garnish with fresh basil.

Grilled Panini with Roasted Red Peppers and Smoked Mozzarella
Serves 4. Prep time: 30 minutes.

8 slices crusty Italian, semolina, or ciabatta bread, or ciabatta rolls
1 pound fresh smoked mozzarella, sliced
1 jar (8 to 10 ounces) roasted peppers, drained
2 tablespoons green salad olives with pimentos, sliced
Extra virgin olive oil for brushing

Make 4 sandwiches with the bread, cheese, roasted peppers, and a few of the olives: keep in single layers.

Heat a nonstick griddle pan over medium heat; or, use a grill. Wrap a brick with foil and place on the top of the panini to weight it down. Grill each sandwich on each side about three minutes, or until golden and the cheese starts to melt.

Italian Sausage and Peppers

Serves 8. Prep time: 30 minutes.

3 pounds Italian sweet or hot sausage (turkey or chicken can be substituted)
2 green bell peppers, seeded and cut into ½" strips
2 red bell peppers, seeded and cut into ½" strips
2 yellow bell peppers, seeded and cut into ½" strips
2 medium red or yellow onions, halved and cut into thin slices
1 medium fennel bulb, top cut off, halved, and cut into thin slices
Balsamic vinegar to drizzle
Fresh Italian rolls, cut in half, brushed with olive oil, and grilled

Heat grill to medium-hot. Butterfly each sausage to open up the middle. Place over the hottest part of the grill and cook well. Turn over after about 12 minutes and cook though on both sides.

While the sausages are cooking, in a hot skillet, on the medium-hot side of your grill, cook the bell peppers, onion, and fennel in extra virgin olive oil until vegetables are soft.

Season with salt and pepper to taste. Drizzle with balsamic vinegar. Add the sausages to the skillet when done and cook for a few minters more so that the flavors can meld with the peppers and onions.

Take a grilled Italian roll and put a healthy spoonful of the sausage and pepper mix in it. Season more to taste. Eat and enjoy!

Mozzarella en Carrozza – **Mozzarella Grilled Cheese**
Makes 6 sandwiches. Prep time: 30 minutes.

2 fresh mozzarella balls, 12 ounces each
4 eggs, beaten
1½ cups Italian bread crumbs
1½ cups all-purpose flour
4 cups grape seed or vegetable oil
Sea salt and freshly ground black pepper
12 slices white or whole wheat bread, cut into circles (with or without crust)
½ cup sun-dried tomatoes in oil, chopped

Cut mozzarella into thin slices lengthwise. Beat eggs in a large bowl and season with salt and pepper. Fill another large bowl with flour, and a third bowl with bread crumbs.

In a deep cast-iron or non-stick sauté pan, pour one-third to one inch oil and heat on medium. When a drop of the egg mixture sizzles, the oil is ready.

Spread a teaspoon of sun-dried tomatoes on each slice of bread. Place a slice of mozzarella on one slice of bread then cover with another slice of bread to make the sandwich. Dip sandwiches into flour, then eggs, and lastly bread crumbs, making sure to coat evenly. Place on a small sheet pan until ready to fry.

When the oil is ready, place a few of the cheese sandwiches in the hot oil and let fry for about one minute on each side, until cheese is melted and the bread is golden brown. Remove with a slotted spoon and place on a baking sheet with a stack of paper towels to dry.

As an extra flavor treat, serve with caramelized onions and fig jam.

Music is the language of the spirit. It opens the secret life of bringing peace, abolishing strife. ~Kahlil Gibran

My Favorite Pasta Dishes

SOMEONE TOLD ME that the pasta consumption in the U.S. is 18.4 pounds per person (1990). In Italy, the average is 60 pounds per person! One should eat about three grams of carbohydrates per pound of body weight each day. Between 55 and 70 percent of all calories should come from carbohydrates.

Southern Italians, it is said, became the masters of homemade pastas. The warm, dry climate in the south favored the drying of freshly made pasta, cooked *al dente* ("to the tooth," i.e., requires chewing).

Specialità

Every so often, a recipe comes along at a party or a special event that you just have to have for yourself. In this section I've included some of those recipes. Recipes that have been in the family for many years have a lot of good in them. When we share these cherished dishes, it's like opening a box of the family jewels and giving each guest a sample to enjoy for a little while. That's what *specialità* is all about. Enjoy these gems, from our family to yours. If you don't have a special occasion, make one up! After all, life is to enjoy every day—and every day is a special event.

Types of Pasta

Bucatini are long, thick pasta.

Cannelloni are hollowed-out pasta tubes in the shape of "bagpipes," usually filled with tomato sauce.

Capellini (also called *fedilini* or *spaghettini*) is "fine-hair" pasta, usually coiled. Angel Hair is even thinner.

Cresti di Galli is named for its resemblance to a "rooster's comb."

Ditalini are small macaroni cut into "little thimble" shapes.

Farfalle, known as bows in this country, look like "butterflies."

Funghini, used in soup, is in pasta's "mushroom" family.

Gnocci are little "dumpling-like" pastas.

Lumache resemble a "snail shell."

Occhi di Lupo are large tubes of macaroni, referred to as "wolf's eyes."

Orcchiette are shaped to resemble "ears."

Pulcini, used in soup, is from the "little chicken" family of pasta.

Ravioli are small cases of pasta, usually stuffed with meat, cheese, or vegetables.

Riccini are groove pasta, twisted into ringlet "curls."

Ruoti are round with spokes, resembling a "chariot wheel."

Tortellini are small rounds of stuffed pasta twisted into a shape resembling the Roman goddess Venus' navel.

Vermicelli is the southern Italian word for spaghetti and means "worms."

Zitti are a type of tubular macaroni "cut" into shorter lengths, often baked in tomato sauce.

Note: You can substitute gluten-free pasta for most of these recipes.

Ravioli with Brown Butter and Sage
Serves 4. Prep time: 30 minutes.

24 ounces fresh cheese ravioli
6 tablespoons unsalted butter
2 medium shallots, thinly sliced
16 fresh sage leaves
¼ teaspoon kosher salt
¼ teaspoon freshly ground black pepper
¾ cup fresh, grated parmesan cheese

In a pot of boiling salted water, cook the ravioli according to directions. Drain and return to the pot.

In a sauté pan over low heat, melt some butter. Add some of the sage leaves and cook until the sage is infused into the butter, about 1½ minutes. Remove from heat.

Add some freshly grated parmesan cheese and season with salt and pepper. Place ravioli into the sauce pan and cover with the brown butter sage sauce.

Serve each person three or four ravioli and garnish with a sage leave and some more parmesan cheese.

Pasta con le Sarde Bucatini – **Pasta with Sardines and Fennel**

Serves 6. Prep time: 30 minutes.

8 ounces sardines packed in oil, well drained
1 pound bucatini pasta
4 cloves garlic, minced
1 cup Italian bread crumbs
⅓ cup parmesan or pecorino cheese
¼ cup Italian flat-leave parsley, chopped
Sea salt and freshly ground pepper to taste
2 lemons, cut into circles
1 medium bulb fennel, cut into long strips
½ cup currants or sultana raisins, soaked until soft

In a pot of boiling, salted water, cook bucatini pasta *al dente*. Drain, coat with olive oil, cover to keep warm, and set aside.

In a sauté pan, cook the garlic in olive oil for 2 minutes, then add the sardines and cook 1 minute more. Add the bread crumbs, cheese, fennel strips, and currants or raisins, and cook until fennel is soft, about 2 more minutes. Stir in the remaining olive oil and parsley along with the red pepper flakes.

Place the bucatini pasta in a small casserole dish and top with the bread crumb mixture. Place the lemon rounds on the top and bake in a 350° oven for about 20 minutes, or until the bread crumbs and lemon rounds are golden. Serve with Pinot Grigio wine.

Linguine and Clams with San Marzano Tomatoes

Serves 6. Prep time: 30 minutes.

1 pound linguine pasta
24 littleneck clams, scrubbed well
5 garlic cloves, thinly sliced
2 teaspoons red pepper flakes, divided
1 cup dry white wine
Sea salt and freshly ground black pepper
1 can (14 ounces) San Marzano tomatoes, diced or chopped
4 sprigs Italian flat-leave parsley, chopped

In a large pot of boiling, salted water, cook pasta *al dente*. Drain, reserving one cup of the pasta water. Set aside.

In a large sauté pan on low heat, add olive oil and garlic; sauté until golden. Add the clams, 1 teaspoon red pepper flakes, white wine, tomatoes with their juice, and parsley. Cover and simmer until the clams open, about 8 minutes. Discard any clams that do not open.

Add the drained pasta to the pan with the reserved water, tossing the pasta until well coated. Remove from heat and add the remaining red pepper flakes, salt, and pepper to taste. Add the rest of the parsley and drizzle with more olive oil. Place a hearty serving on each plate and enjoy!

Salsa di Noci – **Fusilli Pasta with Walnut Pesto and Cheese**
Makes 1½ quarts. Prep time: 30 minutes.

1 cup whole or chopped walnuts
2 cups baby spinach
2 cups baby arugula
15 ounces whole-milk ricotta cheese
3 whole garlic cloves
Sea salt and freshly ground black pepper to taste
½ cup extra virgin olive oil
1 cup grated parmesan & pecorino mix
1 wedge asiago cheese for shaving
1 pound pasta (suggested pasta: fusilli, casarecce, cavatelli, gemelli, ravioli, and/or rotelli)

In a 7-cup food processor, place the walnuts, garlic cloves, spinach, arugula, cheese, salt, and pepper. While pulsing, add the olive oil slowly until the mixture gets smooth.

In a medium bowl, place the ricotta cheese. Add the mixture from the processor and fold all together until blended well. Taste and adjust seasoning as needed. Cover and refrigerate until ready to use.

Cook pasta *al dente* and toss in with the Walnut Pesto.

Shave asiago cheese on the top in wide shavings. Serve in separate bowls topped with walnut pieces.

Jumbo Shells with Mozzarella, Mascarpone, and Parmigiana Cheese
Serves 8. Prep time: 40 minutes.

1 box (16 ounces) jumbo pasta shells
24 ounces marinara sauce
2 cups whole-milk ricotta cheese
8 ounces mascarpone cheese
1 cup freshly grated Parmigiana cheese
8 ounces mozzarella cheese, shredded
1 egg, beaten
¼ cup chopped Italian parsley
Sea salt and black pepper to taste

Preheat oven to 400°. Cook shells in boiling, salted water for about 10 minutes, leaving them *al dente*. Drain under cold water and place on baking sheet to cool.

In a glass or metal bowl, mix together ricotta, mascarpone, half of the Parmigiano, half of the mozzarella, parsley, salt, and pepper. Fill each shell with the cheese mixture.

Coat the bottom of a 9" x 13" baking dish with marinara sauce. Arrange the shells side by side, with the opening facing upward, until the baking dish is filled. Pour the remaining sauce over them and top with remaining mozzarella and Parmigiana cheese.

Cover baking dish with aluminum foil and bake for about 30 minutes, or until cheese starts to bubble.

Gnocchetti con Trevisana – **Gnocchi with Radicchio**
Serves 4. Prep time: 30 minutes.

1 head Treviso radicchio, or common radicchio
2 tablespoons unsalted butter
1 cup heavy cream or half-and-half
3 tablespoons marinara sauce
1 pound potato gnocchi
3 ounces hard provolone cheese, grated

Wash the radicchio and cut into thin strips. Melt butter in a skillet and sauté the radicchio until wilted. Stir in the cream and cook until reduced. Fold in the marinara sauce and salt to taste.

In a large pot of boiling, salted water, cook gnocchi until they rise to the surface. Remove with a slotted spoon and place into four separate buttered baking dishes. Spoon the radicchio and sauce over the top. Sprinkle with the provolone and place under a preheated broiler until cheese melts, about 8 minutes. Take out and let cool for 1 minute before serving.

Spinach Mushroom Lasagna with Italian Chicken Sausage and Black Olives
Makes two 9" x 15" casseroles. Prep time: 60 minutes

16 ounces no-boil lasagna noodles, plus a few extra noodles
12 ounces shredded light mozzarella cheese
2 eggs
10 ounces white or cremini mushrooms
26 ounces marinara sauce
2 cups baby spinach
3 pounds whole-milk ricotta
16 ounces black olives
3 tablespoons pecorino cheese
8 Italian chicken sausage breakfast links
½ cup chopped Italian parsley
Sea salt and freshly ground black pepper

Preheat the oven to 375°.

In a large mixing bowl, combine the ricotta cheese, two eggs, chopped parsley, ¾ cup shredded mozzarella, salt, and black pepper. Mix well.

In the bottom of the two casserole dishes, spread a few spoons of marinara sauce. Place four of the no-boil noodles on the marinara in each dish, covering the whole bottom of the dish. Put a few tablespoons of the ricotta cheese mixture on each noodle and spread it evenly. Put a few of the baby spinach leaves on each noodle and cover with some of the sautéed mushrooms. Add a few chopped olives to each noodle and cover with four more noodles.

Repeat the above process until you have three layers.

Top with enough chopped sausage links to entirely cover the noodles, then cover all with the rest of the mozzarella cheese and sprinkle the Pecorino cheese over all. Cover with aluminum foil and place in oven.

Cook for about 1 hour, until the noodles are soft and the cheese bubbles. For a crusty noodle, remove the foil and bake a few more minutes in the oven. Let cool a bit before serving.

Roasted Red Pepper Coulee
Serves 12. Prep time: 20 minutes.

4 red bell peppers
¼ cup chicken stock
3 teaspoons olive oil
Salt and pepper to taste

Cut and core the bell peppers. Place on a baking sheet and drizzle with olive oil. Roast in 350° oven or char over gas flame until done.

Remove from heat and place in a paper bag to cool. When cool enough to handle, peel the peppers, discard the seeds, and place peppers in the blender. Add chicken stock and blend to a smooth sauce. Season to taste with salt and black pepper.

Orecchiette Pasta with Roasted Garlic and Vine-ripe Roma Tomatoes in a Mild Gorgonzola Cream Sauce
Serves 6-8. Prep time: 30 minutes.

1 pound orecchiette pasta
1 cup Gorgonzola cheese
6 vine-ripe Roma tomatoes, cut into quarters
4 garlic cloves, roasted
1 pint heavy cream or half-and-half
Salt and freshly ground black pepper
Red pepper flakes or dried chili peppers (optional)
Extra virgin olive oil
½ cup basil chiffonade
½ cup Italian parsley, chopped

Slice the tomatoes and peel the garlic. Place on a baking sheet, drizzle with olive oil, and sprinkle with salt and pepper. Place into 350° oven to roast until done.

In a saucepan, whisk the cream on high heat until almost bubbling; then lower the heat, add the Gorgonzola cheese, and whisk until smooth. Season with salt and black pepper.

Cook the pasta *al dente* and toss in sauce. Serve in pasta bowls.

Fusilli with Roasted Eggplant, Roma Tomatoes, Pine Nuts, and Currants
Serves 8. Prep time: 45 minutes.

1 pound fusilli or casarecce pasta
2 medium eggplants, cut crosswise into ½" slices
3 tablespoons olive oil
1 medium onion, chopped
4 garlic cloves, minced
¾ cup pine nuts, toasted
¾ cup currants
1 pint half-and-half
3 cups Roma tomatoes, cut into quarters and roasted
½ cup freshly-grated Pecorino-Romano cheese
½ cup chopped fresh basil
Salt and freshly ground black pepper
Red pepper flakes

Place eggplant slices on a large, rimmed baking sheet. Sprinkle with salt. Let stand 20 minutes. Turn eggplants slices over. Sprinkle with salt. Let stand 20 minutes longer. Rinse eggplant. Drain; pat dry with paper towels. Cut eggplant into ½" cubes. Set aside.

Heat olive oil in a heavy, large skillet over medium heat. Add onion and sauté until golden, about 4 minutes. Add garlic; sauté 1 minute. Add eggplant; sauté until tender, about 10 minutes. (Eggplant can also be covered with olive oil and salt, placed on a baking sheet with the Roma tomatoes, and roasted in a 350° oven for about 45 minutes.)

Stir in pine nuts and currants. Sauté 1 minute. Season to taste with salt and pepper. Add half-and-half and cook for a few more minutes over medium flame.

Cook pasta *al dente*. Drain, return pasta to pot. Transfer to a large bowl. Toss the eggplant, tomatoes, pine nuts, currants, cream sauce, and cheese with the pasta. Add salt, pepper, and red pepper flakes to taste. Add fresh basil. Mix well.

***Pasta Rigoletto del Mar ala Verdura* – Capellini with Shrimp and Asparagus**
Serves 4. Prep time: 30 minutes.

1 pound shrimp (medium-sized; cleaned and peeled)
1 medium onion, chopped
2 cloves garlic, minced
2 tablespoons extra virgin olive oil
2 cups fresh or canned plum tomatoes, chopped
1 teaspoon fresh thyme leaves
½ teaspoon red pepper flakes
1 pound asparagus
1 pound capellini (angel hair) pasta
2 tablespoons Italian parsley, chopped

In a skillet, soften the onion and garlic in olive oil. Add tomatoes, thyme, and pepper flakes, and simmer gently, covered, for 15 minutes. Add water if the sauce gets too thick.

Cut the asparagus spears into 2" pieces. Place in a steamer and steam until bright green.

Boil the water and cook the pasta *al dente*. Add the shrimp to the sauce and cook for 2 minutes. Add asparagus and cook for 1 more minute. Place in heated bowl and mix everything together.

Serve and sing!

Turkey Bolognese over Pappardelle
Serves 6. Prep time: 30 minutes.

1 pound fresh pappardelle pasta
3 garlic cloves, peeled and coarsely chopped
1 medium sweet onion, coarsely chopped
1 celery stalk, coarsely chopped
1 medium carrot, coarsely chopped
¼ cup extra virgin olive oil
1 pound ground turkey
28 ounce can crushed San Marzano tomatoes
½ cup Italian flat-leaf parsley, chopped
10 fresh basil leaves, broken
Kosher or sea salt and freshly ground black pepper
¼ cup freshly grated parmesan cheese

In a large porcelain cooking pot with lid, heat the olive oil to almost smoking. Add the onion and garlic; cook until the onions become soft, about 6 minutes. Add the celery and carrots and cook for 5 more minutes.

Add the seasoned ground turkey, stirring to break up any lumps. Cook until meat is browned, about 5 minutes. Season to taste. Add the tomatoes and cook for 5 to 7 more minutes on low.

Boil pappardelle *al dente*, about 10 minutes. Place pasta in the pot with the Bolognese sauce. Top with parmesan cheese, Italian parsley, and basil. Toss well and serve.

Penne Pasta with Sicilian Sausage

Serves 6. Prep time: 30 minutes.

16 ounces penne pasta
1 red bell pepper, cut into strips
1 green bell pepper, cut into strips
¼ cup red wine
4 garlic cloves, minced
1 medium sweet onion, chopped
 8 fresh basil leaves, broken
¼ cup balsamic vinegar
¼ cup Pecorino Romano cheese
Sea salt and freshly ground black pepper
6 Sicilian chicken sausages out of the casings

Cook penne pasta *al dente*, about 10 minutes, in boiling, salted water. Drain and set aside.

In a cast iron skillet or medium sauté pan with olive oil, add the onion and sauté until translucent. Add the sausage and cook over medium heat until all the pink is gone from the meat.

In another skillet, add some olive oil and cook the bell peppers over medium heat for 6 to 8 minutes. Reduce the heat and add the balsamic vinegar. Season with salt & pepper. Add the chopped tomatoes and some of the basil; let simmer a few more minutes. Season again to taste.

In a large pasta bowl or serving bowl, toss together pasta with sausage and sauce. Add the Pecorino Romano cheese and some broken basil leaves. Serve in small pasta bowls with cheese sprinkled on the top, and sing!

Dance as though no one is watching you; love as though you have never been hurt before; sing as though no one can hear you; live...heaven is on earth. ~Souza

Chicken and Meat Dishes

CHICKEN AS A meat can be traced back to around 600 B.C. It was one of the most common meats in the middle ages. Chicken is a good source of protein. There are many special recipes from all over the world that use chicken, and here are a few of my most-requested recipes.

Academy Awards Braised Chicken Drumsticks in Tomato Sauce with Eggplant, Potatoes, Mushrooms, and Kalamata Olives
Serves 6. Prep time: 60 minutes.

6 chicken drumsticks, about 2½ pounds
1 small Italian eggplant, peeled and chopped
3 celery stalks, chopped
3 carrots, chopped
1 medium sweet onion, chopped
1 small garlic bulb, cloves sliced thin
1 jar (16 ounces) marinara sauce
1 cup cremini or button mushroom, halved
½ cup pitted Kalamata olives, chopped
1 cup small golden potatoes, cut into thin rounds and parboiled
1 sprig rosemary
6 basil leaves
½ cup chopped Italian parsley
1 teaspoon red pepper flakes
½ cup red wine
¼ cup extra virgin olive oil
Kosher salt and ground black pepper to taste
½ cup flour for dredging
1 loaf of Italian bread, cut in half lengthwise with chopped garlic on the top

Preheat oven to 350°.

Wash and pat dry the 6 chicken legs. Sprinkle with salt and pepper, then dredge in flour.

In a cast-iron brasier dish over medium-high heat, cook chicken legs on both sides until golden brown. Remove from pan and set aside.

Lower the heat and add the olive oil, onions, celery, and carrots to the same dish. Sauté until soft. Scrape the bottom of the pan so that all the flavors blend together. Add olive oil and cubed eggplant to the pan; cook until soft, stirring so eggplant does not stick. Add more olive oil if needed. Season with salt and pepper

Place the chicken legs back in the pan. Cover and lower the heat for a few minutes; then add the red wine, stir, and bring to a boil. Turn off the heat. Cover and place in the heated oven for 45 to 60 minutes.

After 30 minutes, stir in the basil, rosemary sprig, and Italian parsley. Return to oven, and after 10 to 15 minutes, remove from oven and let rest for about 10 minutes.

Place some garlic bread in the heated oven until golden brown and crispy; remove and cut into ¼" slices for dipping.

Serve each person a generous helping with one leg each. Pour some red wine and give yourself an Academy Award for such a memorable performance!

Classic Chicken Marsala
Serves 4. Prep time: 30 minutes.

4 boneless chicken breasts, 6 ounces each
4 ounces imported Prosciutto, chopped
1 cup chicken, veal, or beef stock
¾ cup dry Marsala wine
1 cup flour
2 tablespoons butter
¼ cup extra virgin olive oil
1 teaspoon salt
¼ cup cremini or button mushrooms, cut in half
Salt and black pepper to taste

In a sauté pan, heat olive oil on medium-high until hot. Pat the chicken dry, season with salt and pepper, and dredge in the flour. Add the chicken to sauté pan and cook about 5 minutes on each side, or until cooked through, Remove from pan and keep covered.

To the same pan, add the chopped prosciutto and cook until crispy. Deglaze the pan with Marsala wine and lower the heat to medium low. Add the mushrooms and cook for 3 minutes, then add the stock and reduce for 2 to 3 minutes. Add the butter and stir well over low heat for 2 more minutes.

Place the cooked chicken breasts on a plate. Spoon Marsala sauce with the crispy prosciutto and mushrooms over the chicken. Garnish with parsley sprigs, and serve.

Roman Chicken
Serves 6. Prep Time 30 minutes.

4 skinless chicken breast halves, with ribs
2 skinless chicken thighs, with bones
½ teaspoon salt, plus 1 teaspoon
½ teaspoon freshly ground black pepper, plus 1 teaspoon
¼ cup olive oil
1 red bell pepper, sliced
1 yellow bell pepper, sliced
3 ounces prosciutto, chopped
2 cloves garlic, chopped
1 can (15 ounces) diced tomatoes
½ cup white wine
1 tablespoon fresh thyme leaves
1 teaspoon fresh oregano leaves
½ cup chicken stock
2 tablespoons capers
¼ cup chopped fresh flat-leaf

Season the chicken with ½ teaspoon salt and ½ teaspoon pepper. In a heavy, large skillet, heat the olive oil over medium heat. When the oil is hot, cook the chicken until browned on both sides. Remove from the pan and set aside.

Keeping the same pan over medium heat, add the peppers and prosciutto and cook until the peppers have browned and the prosciutto is crisp, about 5 minutes. Add the garlic and cook for 1 minute. Add the tomatoes, wine, and herbs. Using a wooden spoon, scrape the browned bits off the bottom of the pan. Return the chicken to the pan, add the stock, and bring the mixture to a boil. Reduce the heat and simmer, covered, until the chicken is cooked through, about 20 to 30 minutes.

If serving immediately, add the capers and the parsley. Stir to combine and serve. If making ahead of time, transfer the chicken and sauce to a storage container, cool, and refrigerate. The next day, reheat the chicken to a simmer over medium heat. Stir in the capers and the parsley and serve.

Chicken Scaloppini with Lemon and Capers
Serves 4. Prep time: 30 minutes.

4 skinless, boneless chicken breast halves, about 5 ounces each
½ teaspoon kosher salt
Freshly ground black pepper
2 tablespoons butter
1 tablespoon extra virgin olive oil
½ cup dry white wine
½ cup chicken stock
3 tablespoons lemon juice
2 tablespoons capers, drained
2 tablespoons finely chopped Italian parsley
½ cup flour

Pound chicken to ¼" thickness between sheets of wax paper or plastic wrap. Season with salt and pepper. Dredge in flour.

In a large frying pan, melt butter with olive oil over medium heat. Add chicken and cook 2 minutes. Turn and cook 2 minutes longer, or until white throughout. Remove to a warmed platter. Cover loosely with foil to keep warm.

Pour wine into pan. Add stock and boil until reduced by half, about 2 minutes. Add lemon juice, capers, and parsley. Pour over chicken and serve.

Sicilian Roasted Leg of Lamb with Oven-Roasted Potatoes

Serves 8. Prep time: 40 minutes.

1 leg of lamb, about 7 pounds, trimmed
¾ cup extra virgin olive oil
2 tablespoons crushed red chili flakes
2 tablespoons dried oregano
4 cloves garlic, minced
1 bunch flat-leaf parsley, minced
8 large russet potatoes, peeled and quartered
Kosher salt and freshly ground pepper to taste

Preheat oven to 500°.

In a medium bowl, combine oil, chili flakes, oregano, garlic, salt, and pepper to make a paste. Rub the paste over the surface of the lamb. Set lamb in a large roasting pan and place in the oven. Roast until the lamb is browned, about 30 minutes. Reduce oven temperature to 400° and cover lamb with aluminum foil; continue cooking for 40 minutes. Remove the foil.

Toss the cut potatoes with olive oil and season with salt and pepper; then add the potatoes to the roasting pan and toss with rendered fat. Continue cooking until potatoes are tender and an instant-read thermometer inserted into the thickest part of the lamb reads 140°, about 45-50 minutes more. Let rest for 20 minutes before serving.

Chicken Saltimbocca

Serves 4. Prep time: 15 minutes.

1 cup all-purpose flour, seasoned with salt and pepper
4 chicken breasts, 6 ounces each
4 large slices prosciutto
4 large sage leaves, plus 20 smaller leaves
2 cups plus 4 tablespoons extra virgin olive oil
4 shallots, thinly sliced
½ pound oyster mushrooms, sliced into ¼" pieces
½ cup chicken stock
2 tablespoons butter
1 bunch Italian parsley, chopped to yield ¼ cup

With a meat mallet, pound the chicken breasts to ¼" thickness. Season each breast with salt and pepper and lay 1 sage leaf on each breast. Lay 1 slice prosciutto over each piece and fold in half like a book. Secure the two sides with a toothpick and dredge each breast in the seasoned flour.

In a heavy-bottomed pot with high sides, heat the 2 cups olive oil to 375°. Make sure you have a slotted spoon close by. Working in a few batches, fry the leaves in the oil, removing with the slotted spoon after 30 seconds. Season with salt, set on a plate lined with paper towels to drain, and set aside.

In a 12" - 14" sauté pan, heat the remaining olive oil until smoking. Add the chicken and sauté until golden brown on both sides. Add the shallots and mushrooms and cook until the mushrooms have sweated, about 5 to 6 minutes. Add the chicken stock and cook over high heat until reduced by half. Swirl the butter into the pan, add the parsley, and serve on 4 warmed dinner plates, topped with the fried sage leaves.

***Braciola alla Marinara* – Stuffed Flank Steaks in Marinara Sauce**
Serves 4. Prep time: 60 minutes.

For the sauce:
52 ounces crushed tomatoes (San Marzano canned tomatoes work well)
3 cloves garlic, peeled and finely chopped
4 teaspoons extra virgin olive oil
2 sprigs fresh oregano, chopped
6 fresh basil leaves, chopped
Salt and freshly ground black pepper

Put tomatoes, garlic, oil, and 1 cup water into a large saucepan and simmer over medium heat, stirring until the sauce thickens slightly, about 15 minutes. Add herbs; season to taste with salt and pepper. Set aside.

For the meat:
6 sprigs fresh basil
4 pieces veal or beef top round, about 8 ounces each, pounded to ¼" thickness
4 ounces thinly sliced prosciutto
1 teaspoon garlic powder or fresh chopped garlic
Salt and freshly ground black pepper
4 teaspoons toasted pine nuts, finely chopped
2 hard-boiled eggs, peeled and finely chopped
2 teaspoons raisins or currants
4 cloves garlic, peeled and finely chopped
4 teaspoons freshly grated parmesan cheese
¼ cup extra virgin olive oil
2 sprigs parsley, chopped

Combine pine nuts, eggs, raisins, garlic, basil, and cheese in a large bowl.

Working with one piece at a time, put meat on a clean surface with narrow end facing you. Season with garlic powder, salt, and pepper to taste. Lay a thin slice of ham on the steak, then scatter ¼ of the pine nut mixture over it, leaving about ½" border on either side. Fold long sides of meat over filling, meeting in the center. Roll up tightly to form a braciola, and tie securely with kitchen twine. Repeat with remaining steaks.

Heat oil in a medium, heavy-bottomed pot with tight-fitting lid over medium-high heat. Add braciole and brown 5 minutes. Add sauce, scraping browned bits stuck to bottom of pot with wooden spoon. Season to taste with salt and pepper and bring to a simmer. Cover pot, reduce heat to medium-low, and gently simmer, turning braciole occasionally, until very tender, about 1½ hours for veal or about 3 hours for beef.

Transfer braciole to a cutting board; cut off and discard twine. Slice crosswise and transfer to 4 warm plates. Spoon sauce on and around braciola and garnish with parsley and remaining basil.

Chicken Cutlets, Italian Style
Serves 4. Prep time: 30 minutes.

4 free range chicken breasts, 6 ounces each
2 eggs, beaten
½ cup Italian bread crumbs
½ cup all-purpose flour
2 cups olive oil or vegetable oil
Sea salt and freshly ground black pepper
2 medium lemons

Season chicken breasts with salt and pepper on both sides.

Fill a bowl with flour, another with beaten eggs, and a third with the bread crumbs.

Pour 1" oil into a deep, cast-iron skillet. Heat the skillet until the oil is hot enough that a drop of water sizzles, but not so hot that it smokes.

Dredge each chicken breast in the flour, then egg, then bread crumbs, making sure that both sides are covered, and place in the heated oil. Let fry for about 2 minutes, until golden brown; then turn over and brown the other side. Drain on a paper towel.

Put each breast on a plate and squeeze some lemon juice on the top of each one. Serve with sautéed mushrooms, buttered fresh green beans, and slices of fresh tomato.

God sent his singers upon the earth / With songs of sadness and mirth,
That they may touch the hearts of men / And bring them back to heaven again.
~Henry Wadsworth Longfellow

Fish and Shellfish

SINCE THE WORLD is mostly made up of water, about 70%, we should indulge in what the wonderful and various bodies of water have to offer. From the fresh water lakes to the bays and the grand oceans, we have been given an *abbondanza*, abundance, of sea life to enjoy.

In Sicily, where my Nonna Grace grew up, there were always fresh fish and shellfish right off the boat. She brought some of her wonderful seafood recipes with her to America, and later shared them with us, her family. I hope you will enjoy some of the following dishes—and maybe even add your own special "hook" to them.

Spaghetti with Fresh Clams, Parsley, and Lemon
Serves 4. Prep time: 30 minutes.

1 pound spaghetti
8 garlic cloves
½ cup extra virgin olive oil
3 pounds fresh manila clams or small littleneck clams, scrubbed
¼ cups plus 2 tablespoons chopped fresh Italian parsley
½ cup dry white wine
¼ cup fresh lemon juice

Heat oil in heavy large pot over medium heat. Add sliced garlic and sauté until light brown, about 1 minute. Add clams and ¼ cup chopped Italian parsley; stir 2 minutes. Add wine; simmer 2 minutes. Add fresh lemon juice. Cover and simmer until clams open, about 6 minutes. Discard clams that do not open.

Cook pasta *al dente*. Drain. Add pasta to the clam mixture and toss to coat. Season to taste with salt and pepper. Transfer to large bowl. Sprinkle with remaining 2 tablespoons parsley and serve.

Red Clam Sauce over Linguine
Serves 4. Prep time: 30 minutes.

1 pound linguine pasta
¼ cup extra virgin olive oil
⅔ cup dry white wine
½ teaspoon dried thyme
½ teaspoon red pepper flakes
3 cups canned crushed tomatoes in thick purée (or use a 28-ounce can)
1 cup bottled clam juice
1¼ teaspoon salt, plus more if needed
¾ pound (about 1½ cups) chopped clams, drained
⅓ cup chopped flat-leaf parsley
¼ teaspoon freshly ground black pepper

In a large sauté pan, heat olive oil over low heat. Add garlic and cook for 1 minute. Add the wine, thyme, and red pepper flakes and bring to a simmer. Cook until reduced to ⅓ cup.

Add tomatoes, clam juice, and salt to taste. Raise the heat and bring to a simmer. Cook, stirring continually, until thickened, about 10 minutes. Add the clams and bring back to a simmer. Cook until clams are just done. Taste the sauce and adjust seasoning as necessary.

Cook pasta in boiling, salted water for 12 minutes. Drain. Toss with the sauce and serve.

Roasted Halibut with Fennel and Potatoes
Serves 4. Prep time: 30 minutes.

4 pieces skinless halibut fillets (about 6 ounces each)
1 pound Yukon Gold potatoes, unpeeled, thinly sliced
1 medium bulb fennel, cored and thinly sliced
1 large leek
2 tablespoons anise-flavored liquor or white wine
2 tablespoons extra virgin olive oil
1 teaspoon fennel seeds
1 lemon, thinly sliced
Fennel fronds for garnish
Salt and black pepper to taste

Heat the oven to 350°.

Cut off roots and trim dark green top from leek. Thinly slice. Rinse in a bowl of water to remove all the sand. Drain well.

In a medium bowl, put in the thinly sliced potatoes and toss them with olive oil and season with salt and pepper. Place in the oven for about 5 to 10 minutes until they soften and brown.

Remove potatoes from the oven. Place halibut on the potatoes and drizzle with anise liquor and oil. Sprinkle with fennel seeds, salt, and pepper. Place lemon slices on top of halibut and return the dish to oven. Roast 10 to 12 minutes or until fish is opaque.

Serve with fennel fronds.

Spicy Shrimp in White Wine and Garlic Butter over Penne Pasta
Serves 6. Prep time: 30 Minutes.

1 pound medium to large shrimp, shelled and de-veined
1 cup flour
1 pound penne pasta
¼ cup garlic butter (recipe below)
¼ cup minced shallots
½ cup dry white wine
½ cup Limoncello (Italian liqueur)
Salt and freshly ground black pepper
Cajon Spice or cayenne pepper
2 tablespoons parsley, finely chopped

Clean and prepare the shrimp.

Season the flour with Cajon Spice or cayenne pepper.

Dredge the shrimp in the seasoned flour.

In a large sauté pan, over medium heat, melt the garlic butter. Add the shrimp and sauté until golden, about 5 minutes. Add the shallots and sauté for 1 minute more. Add the wine and simmer for 2 minutes until reduced. Add Limoncello; flame. Stir in the parsley. Remove from heat and serve over pasta or rice.

Garlic Butter

2 sticks unsalted butter, brought to room temperature
¼ cup finely chopped garlic
Kosher salt and white pepper

In a mixing bowl, combine all ingredients together and mix well. Store butter in a ramekin and cover with plastic wrap until ready to use.

Shrimp Scampi
Serves 6. Prep time: 30 minutes.

1 pound medium shrimp, peeled and deveined
½ cup unsalted butter
1 cup Pinot Grigio wine or dry white wine
5 cloves minced garlic
1 pound capellini (angel hair) pasta
2 sprigs flat-leaf Italian parsley, chopped
¾ cup fresh, grated parmesan cheese
Sea salt and freshly ground pepper to taste
1 teaspoon red pepper flakes

In a pot of boiling, salted water, cook capellini *al dente*. Drain and set aside.

In a sauté pan over low heat, melt the butter. Stir in the garlic, then add the shrimp. Do not to overcook the shrimp. Add white wine and red pepper flakes and cook for about 1 minute.

In a large bowl, combine the capellini and shrimp. Toss with the cheese and add the chopped parsley. Add some ground black pepper if desired.

Mussels in Red Sauce
Serves 6. Prep time: 30 minutes.

1½ pounds mussels, scrubbed and cleaned well
3 cups diced organic plum tomatoes
3 garlic cloves, minced
1 shallot, minced
2 tablespoons capers
1 tablespoon unsalted butter
¼ cup extra virgin olive oil
2 sprigs Italian flat-leave parsley
1 teaspoon crushed red pepper flakes

In a sauté pan, melt the butter over low heat and add the olive oil. Add the garlic, capers, and shallots and cook until translucent.

Add the diced tomatoes and red pepper flakes. Cover, reduce heat, and cook for a few more minutes.

Add the mussels to the pan and cover tightly. Cook until the mussels have opened. Discard the ones that do not open. Remove from heat and place in small bowls. Garnish with the fresh parsley and serve with small forks.

Baked Clams with Oregano and Italian Breadcrumbs

Serves 8. Prep time: 30 minutes.

2 dozen littleneck clams, scrubbed well
2 cups red onion, diced
5 garlic cloves, sliced thin
3 cups sea salt
¼ cup extra virgin olive oil
1 red or yellow bell pepper, cut into ⅛" slices
1 cup Italian bread crumbs
3 tablespoons chopped fresh oregano
¼ cup fresh parmesan cheese

Open the clams and drain the liquid into a mixing bowl. Set aside. Loosen each clam from its shell, but do not remove. Pour the sea salt onto a baking sheet to ½" deep and place each clam on it.

In a 12" sauté pan, heat the olive oil until almost smoking. Add the onion, garlic, and bell pepper, and cook for about 7 minutes. Add the bread crumbs and continue cooking until light golden brown. Remove from heat and season with salt and pepper. Let cool and then stir in the reserved clam juice and oregano.

Preheat the broiler. Spoon 2 tablespoons of the crumb mixture into each clam. Place the clams under the broiler about 2 minutes, or until golden brown. Drizzle with olive oil and parmesan cheese. Serve.

Stuffed Squid, Italian Style
Serves 6. Prep time: 30 minutes.

6 medium squid, cut into tubes and cleaned, reserving tentacles
1 can (15 ounces) San Marzano tomatoes, diced
¼ cup Italian bread crumbs
2 sprigs Italian flat-leave parsley, chopped
3 garlic cloves, minced
¼ cup parmesan cheese
½ teaspoon ground oregano
½ teaspoon ground rosemary
1 red bell pepper, diced
Sea salt and freshly ground black pepper
3 basil leaves, chopped
¼ cup dry white wine
1 egg, beaten
2 cups marinara sauce

Cut and clean the squid. Chop the tentacles and mix with breadcrumbs, parsley, cheese, beaten egg, minced garlic, and olive oil in a medium bowl. Season with salt and pepper and mix well.

Spoon the stuffing mixture loosely into each squid shell. Do not overstuff, as the squid will shrink some. Secure with a toothpick. In a saucepan with olive oil, place the stuffed squid tubes in single layer and brown on both sides until golden brown.

Add tomatoes, basil, oregano, rosemary, white wine, and garlic; cover tightly and cook for 25 to 30 minutes. Spoon tomato sauce on each plate, then put the squid on top, whole or cut into medallions.

Sea Bass in *Cartoccio* (Parchment Paper)
Serves 4. Prep time: 40 minutes.

4 fillets of sea bass (or salmon), 6 ounces each
1 small yellow squash, julienned
2 medium carrots, peeled and julienned
1 bulb fresh fennel, julienned
10 leaves Swiss or rainbow chard, trimmed and chiffonade
4 branches fresh oregano
1 bunch Italian parsley, chopped
12 Kalamata or Gaeta olives, chopped
1 cup white wine
¼ cup extra virgin olive oil
Sea salt and black pepper to taste
Juice of 1 lemon

Cut parchment paper into 12" squares. Preheat oven to 450°.

Season the fish fillets with salt and pepper.

Mix all the vegetables in a large bowl. Season and toss well. Divide the mixed vegetables into 4 portions and place one portion in the center of each of the parchment paper squares. Place one of the fillets on top of the vegetables, and top off with one branch of oregano.

Divide the parsley, olives, and white wine over each fish fillet, and add a drizzle of olive oil. Fold up each packet and seal the edges by folding them over several times.

Bake in a 450° oven for 12 to 14 minutes. Open up in front of each guest; sprinkle with lemon juice and garnish with fennel fronds.

Muscioli al Forno – **Baked Mussels**
Serves 6. Prep time: 30 minutes.

3 pounds fresh mussels, washed and scrubbed
1 pound ripe tomatoes, chopped
¼ cup Italian bread crumbs
4 teaspoons extra virgin olive oil
3 sprigs Italian parsley, chopped
Salt and pepper

Wash mussels several times with salt water, cleaning with a stiff brush, making sure to remove the beards and all sand. Open them with knife; or, sauté in a pan with olive oil until they open. Remove the mussel and put two or three on each half shell. Arrange them side by side in a large shallow baking dish.

Rub the tomatoes through a fine sieve. Mix together tomato pulp, bread crumbs, parsley, olive oil, salt, and pepper. Spread a bit of mixture on top of the mussels and bake at 350° for 10 to 15 minutes, until they are lightly browned. Serve.

Grilled Baby Tuna Steaks with Toasted Almond-Basil Pesto
Serves 4. Prep time: 40 minutes.

4 tuna, shark, or swordfish steaks, about 6 ounces each and ¼" thick
25 large fresh basil leaves
4 garlic cloves
¼ cup whole almonds, toasted
¾ pound plum tomatoes, peeled, seeded, chopped, and drained
3 tablespoons extra virgin olive oil
¼ cup cracked green olives, pitted and chopped
4 tablespoons dry white bread crumbs
2 pounds fresh baby spinach

For Salmoriglio (Sicilian marinade sauce):
½ cup extra virgin olive oil
¼ cup fresh lemon juice
2 tablespoons hot water
6 tablespoons fresh parsley, chopped
3 large garlic cloves, finely chopped
1 tablespoon dried oregano
Salt and pepper to taste

Whisk olive oil in top of double boiler over simmering water until heated through. Gradually whisk in fresh lemon juice, then 2 tablespoons of water. Add parsley, garlic, and oregano. Cook sauce 5 minutes over low heat to blend flavors, whisking frequently. Season with salt and pepper.

With food processor running, drop in garlic and process until chopped. Add basil and almonds and chop finely. Add tomatoes, oil, and olives; pulse until mix resembles paste. Season with salt and pepper.

Preheat oven to 400°, or make sure your grill is ready to go. Lightly oil a large baking sheet. Arrange the fish on the baking sheet side by side and sprinkle with salt and pepper. Grill or bake the fillets on both sides until transparent. When done, spread some of the pesto on top and place under the broiler for a few minutes to toast the bread crumb topping.

Cook the spinach in olive oil and garlic until wilted. Put on a plate and put the fish steaks on the top. Spoon Salmoriglio sauce over fish and serve.

Grilled Halibut with Saffron-Orange Aioli in Soft Tortillas
Serves 6. Prep time: 30 minutes.

4 fillets of halibut, 6 ounces each
6 flour or corn tortillas
1 large egg yolk
¾ cup olive oil
⅛ teaspoon saffron
1 tablespoon hot water
1 clove garlic, chopped
1 teaspoon orange zest
¼ cup freshly squeezed orange juice
1 teaspoon freshly squeezed lemon juice
¾ teaspoon salt
¼ teaspoon black pepper

To make the aioli, combine saffron and water in a food processor. Add remaining ingredients, except olive oil and fish, and pulse until combined. With processor running, slowly add oil until thick and emulsified. Chill.

Over medium-high heat, grill halibut about four minutes on each side, or until opaque in the center. Cut into small bite sized pieces. Serve in warm tortillas, and spoon the aioli over the top. Fold and enjoy!

I used to work in the cotton fields a lot when I was young.
There were a lot of African Americans out there, a lot of Mexicans, the black and the
whites and the Mexicans all singing, and it was like an opera in the cotton fields.
I can still hear it in the music that I write and play today. ~Willie Nelson

Side Dishes

CONTORNO, OR SIDE dishes, should complement the main course that you are serving. They should not overpower what is being featured on the plate, but add to the flavors and textures of the whole experience. You can even have a whole dinner of just side dishes—but make sure you have enough wine to go around!

Polenta with Roasted Peppers, Mushrooms, and Pecorino Cheese
Serves 6. Prep time: 30 minutes.

4 cups water
1 cup polenta
1 bay leaf
Salt and black pepper to taste
½ cup chopped mushrooms, cremini or white button
¼ cup pecorino cheese
1 cup roasted red bell peppers

In a pre-heated oven, at 375°, roast the peppers until done (about 30 minutes). Remove and discard black skin and seeds, chop the peppers, and set aside.

Bring 4 cups of water to a boil; add salt, pepper, and bay leaf. Slowly whisk in polenta. Stir until it sticks to the sides of the pan. Pour polenta into a baking sheet and let cool.

Meanwhile, sauté the chopped mushrooms in olive oil.

When polenta has hardened, cut into 2" to 4" squares or triangles and toast in a sauté pan with olive oil, or roast in the oven until golden. Serve with the roasted peppers and mushrooms, topped with cheese.

Grilled Portobello Mushrooms and Treviso over Creamy Polenta
Serves 4. Prep time: 20 minutes.

4 heads Treviso radicchio
4 portobello mushrooms
6 tablespoons red wine vinegar or aged balsamic vinegar
2 cloves garlic, thinly sliced
4 anchovy fillets, finely chopped
1 bunch marjoram, leaves removed, barely chopped
8 tablespoons extra virgin olive oil

For Creamy Polenta
2 cups cold water
2 cups whole milk
1 cup yellow cornmeal (polenta)
2 ounces mascarpone cheese
Salt and freshly ground black pepper

Preheat grill to medium temperature.

Cut radicchio lengthwise and place in a glass ovenware dish. Clean out the center of the portobello mushrooms and place in the same dish. In a small bowl, mix vinegar, garlic, anchovies, marjoram, and olive oil. Pour over the radicchio and mushrooms and let sit for one hour.

Meanwhile, make the creamy polenta: In a pot over medium heat, bring the water and milk to a boil. Slowly stir in the polenta. Cook, stirring constantly, for 15 minutes. Stir in the mascarpone for a smooth and creamy texture. Season with salt and pepper. Remove from the heat.

Place portobello mushrooms and radicchio on the grill and cook until lightly charred on one side, about 4 to 5 minutes. Dredge in the marinade. Cut mushrooms into strips and place on top of the polenta with the radicchio.

Carciofi Ripiene –Stuffed Artichokes
Serves 8. Prep time: 60 minutes.

4 medium sized artichokes, cut in half lengthwise
1½ cups toasted Italian bread crumbs
½ cup Romano or Pecorino cheese, grated
1 tablespoon pine nuts
1 tablespoon currants
1 onion, chopped
3 sprigs parsley
½ teaspoon sea salt
½ teaspoon pepper
2 tablespoons olive oil

Preheat oven to 375°.

Cut artichokes in half and remove the inner leaves and spines. Steam artichokes until tender, about 40 minutes.

Mix the remaining ingredients in a saucepan and sauté in oil until lightly browned. Pour into a large bowl and season to taste with sea salt and black pepper. Stuff filling into artichokes halves. Put onto a baking sheet and bake 10 to 15 minutes, until the cheese starts to melt and the bread crumbs are toasted.

Homemade Rossini Ricotta Cheese
Makes 6-7 cups. Prep time: 40 minutes.

1 gallon whole milk
1 pint buttermilk (plus more if needed)
1 teaspoon sea salt
Cheesecloth

In a 3 or 4 gallon pot, bring milk and salt to a boil. Start with burner on high, then lower the heat so the milk doesn't scald. Add the buttermilk and stir continually so the milk doesn't stick to the bottom of the pot. Heat slowly to 180°, about 15 minutes. When it reaches this temperature, the milk will slowly thicken and separate into little curds. They will begin to float to the top.

Cut just enough cheesecloth to place over the top of a 2-gallon bowl or pot. Secure the cheesecloth with rubber bands or string so that it doesn't slip into the bowl. Pour the liquid into the cheesecloth very slowly. The curds will stay on the top, and the whey (the clear, yellow liquid) will pass through the cheesecloth into the bowl. (You can refrigerate the whey and drink it cold, or cook your rice in it. It is loaded with many good vitamins.)

To get the maximum amount of cheese, you can bring the whey back to a boil again and pour through the cheesecloth. Continue the process until the whey is very clear.

Remove the cheesecloth with the ricotta and twist into a small ball shape. Place in a bowl and refrigerate overnight.

Use this fresh ricotta as a savory treat on top of crusty bread, in lasagna, or as a filling for cannoli. Combine 2 cups ricotta with ⅔ cup confectioner's sugar in a food processor or blender until creamy and smooth. Stir in small chocolate chips. Use a pastry bag to fill the cannoli shells.

Grilled Eggplant Roulades
Serves 4. Prep time: 30 minutes.

12 slices of eggplant, cut lengthwise (about ¼" thick)
Drizzle of olive oil
Salt and freshly ground black pepper
12 slices prosciutto ham
12 slices fresh mozzarella cheese, about ⅛" thick
1 small head radicchio lettuce
¼ cup of extra virgin olive oil
½ cup Balsamic syrup

Preheat the grill to 375°.

Season both sides of eggplant slices with olive oil, salt, and pepper. Grill the eggplant for 2 minutes on each side.

Lay a piece of prosciutto on one piece of grilled eggplant. Lay a slice of cheese on top of the prosciutto. Carefully roll up the eggplant and secure the roll with two toothpicks. Repeat the above process with the remaining grilled eggplant.

Cut the radicchio in quarters. Toss with olive oil, salt, and pepper. Grill for 1 minute on each side. Remove from the grill and cut away the core of the lettuce. Using a sharp knife, shred the radicchio.

In a mixing bowl, toss the radicchio with olive oil, salt, and pepper. Set aside.

Place the eggplant roulades on the grill and cook until the cheese starts to melt, about 1 minute. Remove from the grill. Place the greens on a large platter. Arrange the roulades on the platter. Drizzle the entire platter with the balsamic syrup.

Nonna's Eggplant Parmesan
Serves 6. Prep time: 30 minutes.

2 medium Italian eggplants, skin removed and cut into thin, even rounds
2 cups Italian bread crumbs
4 eggs, beaten
2 cups flour
16 ounces tomato basil sauce
1 cup extra virgin olive oil
1 cup freshly grated parmesan cheese
2 cups shredded mozzarella cheese
8 leaves of fresh basil, chiffonade
Sea salt and ground black pepper
9" x 15" baking dish (1 extra if needed)

Preheat oven to 350°.

Into two sauté pans (cast-iron is best), pour enough olive oil to cover the bottom.

Beat eggs in a medium bowl. In another bowl, place Italian bread crumbs; in a third bowl, place the flour and season with salt and pepper.

Dredge each round of eggplant in flour, then egg, then bread crumbs, covering both sides of each slice. Place each round in the sauté pan, about 4 pieces in each pan. Brown both sides on low to medium heat.

Cover the bottom of a 9" x 15" glass casserole dish with some tomato sauce, then place fried eggplant rounds in the sauce, covering the bottom of the pan. Repeat the above process until all the eggplant is browned and there are at least 6 stacks of eggplant about three rounds to each stack. Pour the remaining tomato sauce over the top. Top with freshly grated parmesan cheese and shaved mozzarella cheese. Add some fresh basil on top of each round.

Cover with foil and bake for at least one hour. Remove from oven and let stand for a few minutes until set. Serve with fresh garlic bread and sing!

Garlicky Mushrooms

Serves 4. Prep time: 30 minutes.

3 tablespoons extra virgin olive oil
2 garlic cloves, minced
½ teaspoon chili flakes
2 pounds button mushrooms, sliced
4 tablespoons dry white wine
2 tablespoons chopped Italian parsley
2 sprigs fresh rosemary
2 tablespoons butter
Salt and freshly ground black pepper

Heat olive oil in a wide skillet. Add the garlic and chili flakes and cook until aromatic. Add the mushrooms and cook over medium-high heat until soft and browned. Add the wine, parsley, rosemary, salt, and pepper. Lower the heat. Cook 5 more minutes, or until all the moisture in the pan has evaporated. Add in the butter and mix all well.

Creamy Mascarpone Cheese Polenta

Serves 4. Prep time: 40 minutes.

2 cups cold water
2 cups whole milk
1 cup yellow cornmeal (polenta)
2 ounces mascarpone cheese
Salt and freshly ground black pepper

In a pot, over medium heat, bring the water and milk to a boil. Slowly stir in the polenta. Cook, stirring constantly, for 15 minutes. Stir in the cheese. Stir in enough of the cream for a smooth and creamy texture. Season with salt and pepper. Remove from heat and serve immediately.

Stuffed Cubanelle Peppers
Serves 4. Prep time: 30 minutes.

4 medium Cubanelle peppers, tops cut off and seeded
1 pound Italian hot or sweet sausage, meat cut out of the casings
1 small sweet onion, diced
6 garlic cloves, minced
1 can (14 ounces) crushed Roma tomatoes
8 ounces low-sodium chicken stock
¼ cup fresh basil, chopped
1 cup pre-cooked Arborio rice
¼ cup extra virgin olive oil
¼ cup parmesan or Romano cheese, grated
¼ cup grated fresh mozzarella
1 cup marinara sauce
Sea salt and freshly ground black pepper

In a large sauté pan, cook the sausage with the onions on high heat, about 5 minutes, until onions are translucent and sausage is browned. Turn heat to low and add garlic; cook for about 1 minute more. Add crushed tomatoes, chicken stock, and basil; stir well and simmer until mixed well.

In a large bowl, add the cooked rice and all the cheeses. Season and mix well. Taste for seasoning and adjust as necessary. Add the stuffing to the peppers, filling to the top.

Place in an oiled casserole dish and bake in a 350° oven for about 20 minutes, or until peppers are soft and cheese is oozing out. Or, cook in a large sauté pan, covered, for about 5 minutes on low-medium heat.

Serve the peppers on a plate with warm marinara sauce and sprinkle with more parmesan cheese.

Seasonal Julienne Vegetables
Serves 4. Prep time: 30 minutes.

1 cup julienned zucchini
1 cup julienned yellow squash
½ cup julienned carrot
½ cup extra virgin olive oil
4 cloves garlic, minced
1 lemon, juiced
Sea salt and freshly ground pepper to taste

In a medium skillet, add the olive oil garlic and sauté 1 minute. Add the remaining vegetables and sauté until cooked but still firm, 1 to 2 minutes. Add salt and pepper to taste. Squeeze lemon juice over the vegetables; toss and serve.

Roasted Asparagus
Serves 8. Prep time: 20 minutes.

2 pounds medium asparagus, stems broken off
2 tablespoons extra virgin olive oil
½ teaspoon kosher salt
⅛ teaspoon freshly ground black pepper
8 lemon wedges

Preheat oven to 425°.

Place asparagus in a flat baking pan or casserole dish. Drizzle with olive oil and sprinkle with salt and pepper. Turn until evenly coated, then arrange in single layer. Roast 10 to 15 minutes, or until tender when pierced and tips start to brown.

If not serving immediately, cool in pan, cover, and refrigerate. To serve, reheat in a 350° oven for 5 minutes and serve with lemon wedges.

Roasted Garlic Mashed Potatoes
Serves 6. Prep time: 30 minutes; cook time: 1 hour, 10 minutes.

3 bulbs garlic, split in half
3 tablespoons olive oil
2 pounds Yukon Gold potatoes, peeled and diced
1 stick of butter, cubed
½ - ¾ cup heavy cream
Salt and white pepper

Preheat the oven to 450°.

Place the garlic on a pie pan and drizzle with olive oil. Season with salt and pepper. Place in the oven and roast for 35-40 minutes, or until tender and golden brown. Remove from the oven and cool.

Remove the garlic cloves from the bulb and place in a small bowl. Using a fork, mash the garlic until smooth.

Place the potatoes in a pot of salted water and bring to a boil. Reduce the heat to medium and cook the potatoes until fork tender, about 15 minutes. Remove the pan from the heat and drain.

Place the potatoes back in the pot and return to low heat. Stir the potatoes constantly for 2 to 3 minutes to dehydrate them. Remove from the heat.

Add the garlic and butter. Using a hand-held masher, mash the butter and garlic into the potatoes. Add enough cream until desired texture is achieved. Season with salt and pepper.

Escarole is the main ingredient in the Italian-American holiday soup known as Stracciatella. It's also found in Italian wedding soup. It is in the endive family and is believed to be native to Sicily and the Mediterranean region. Today it is grown not only in Italy, France, and Spain, but also Netherlands. Below is one of my favorite uses for this healthy, bitter green.

Escarole and Cannellini Beans
Serves 4. Prep time: 20 Minutes.

2 large heads escarole lettuce
2 cans (16 ounces each) cannellini beans
Sea salt and freshly ground black pepper to taste
3 sprigs Italian flat-leaf parsley, chopped
2 cloves garlic, minced
2 teaspoons crushed red pepper flakes
¼ cup fresh, grated parmesan cheese
Extra virgin olive oil

In a large skillet over medium heat, add some olive oil. Toss in the washed and chopped escarole and coat with the olive oil. Season with salt, pepper, and red pepper flakes. Cook over medium heat for about 10 minutes or until escarole is soft and tender.

In another skillet with olive oil, add the cannellini beans with garlic, salt, and pepper. Simmer until creamy. Add the escarole and parsley and simmer for 10 minutes more. Serve with freshly grated parmesan cheese.

Prosciutto-Wrapped Asparagus
Serves 4. Prep time: 20 minutes.

1 pound fresh asparagus spears, trimmed
1½ pound prosciutto, cut thinly
3 cloves garlic, minced
¼ cup extra virgin olive oil
1 medium lemon
Sea salt and freshly ground black pepper

In steamer pot over low- medium heat, steam the asparagus until tender. Remove the hard stems.

In a sauce pan melt butter and add the olive oil. Wrap each asparagus spear with a slice of the prosciutto ham. Place the wrapped asparagus into the pan and cover. Sauté over medium heat for 2 minutes. Turn each spear over and continue to sauté until fully cooked and prosciutto is crispy.

Remove from pan, season with salt and pepper, and squeeze the juice of one lemon over the spears.

Garlic Broccoli Rabe
Serves 4. Prep time: 20 minutes.

1 bunch small broccoli rabe, each stem cut into 2 or 3 pieces
2 tablespoons extra virgin olive oil
2 cloves garlic, thinly sliced
¼ teaspoon crushed red pepper flakes
½ teaspoon kosher salt
¼ cup pine nuts

Bring large pot of salted water to a boil. Add broccoli rabe and cook 2 or 3 minutes, until firm-tender and bright green. Drain and place in ice bath to stop cooking. When cool, remove the stems.

Clean pot and add olive oil, garlic, pine nuts, and red pepper. Cook over medium heat until garlic is lightly golden, about 2 minutes. Do not burn pine nuts. Add broccoli rabe and salt; cook 2 minutes longer, tossing with tongs until tender. Serve on separate side platter or place with the main course on platter.

Firecracker Stuffed Red Bell Peppers
Serves 10. Prep time: 40 minutes.

5 medium to large red bell peppers, cut in half lengthwise
1½ pounds ground turkey or beef
1½ cups basmati, white, or brown rice, cooked
¼ cup extra virgin olive oil
2 garlic cloves, minced
¼ cup Italian flat-leave parsley, chopped
1 medium sweet onion, chopped
1 cup chopped tomatoes
1 cup tomato-basil sauce
2½ cups shredded mozzarella cheese
1 teaspoon cumin
1 teaspoon ginger powder
1 teaspoon chili powder
1 teaspoon cayenne pepper
¼ cup freshly-grated parmesan cheese for garnish
Sea salt and freshly ground pepper to taste

Preheat oven to 350°.

In cast-iron skillet with lid, add the olive oil, then the ground turkey. Season to taste. Let brown for a few minutes, then add the chopped onion, garlic, parsley, cumin, ginger powder, Italian flat leave parsley, 1 cup chopped tomatoes, chili powder, cayenne pepper, and sea salt and pepper to taste. Mix all well and let simmer in skillet with lid on for about 10 minutes.

Add ½ cup of shredded mozzarella cheese and mix well. Let cool.

Cut the tops off of the red bell peppers, removing the seeds and stems from the inside.

Place in a 9" x 13" baking dish and soften in the oven for about 20 minutes. Let the peppers cool for about 5 minutes. When the peppers are room temperature, stuff each red bell pepper with the filling. Top off with the rest of the shredded mozzarella cheese.

Cover with foil and bake in a 350° oven for 30 minutes. Remove from oven and let cool. To serve, spoon a little tomato sauce, puréed, on a dinner plate, place the pepper on the sauce, and sprinkle with freshly grated parmesan cheese.

Come live, and be merry, and join with me
To sing the sweet chorus of 'Ha ha he!' ~William Blake

La Dolce Vita ~ Desserts

I KNOW WHAT you're thinking: sweets = calories! Okay, but you can eat them in moderation and adjust the recipes to fit your diet - or you can just go for it!

Sweets are very grounding. They have lots of the element of earth in them, and some of us need to be more in touch with the earth, or grounded.

Many celebrations at our house had an abundance of sweets to balance the rest of the flavors: salty, sour, pungent, bitter, and astringent. I find it hard to pass up some mouth-watering desserts; to deny myself would create more stress, so I indulge with moderations. Sometimes I'll go into an Italian restaurant, order just a dessert and a cup of decaf cappuccino, and be in bliss. Don't deny yourself anything in this life that is fun— and desserts are fun. They keep us in mind of celebrations, good times, laughter, and good friends; and good friends always make "good desserts."

You may have tried some of the following desserts, either at home or from a bakery. When they're made fresh, they'll be the hit of the meal or the season. Some of these recipes are made only around the holidays in our family, but you can make them any time the occasion arises. These desserts will make anybody sing!

The Chocolate Meatball Cookies were my favorite, along with the cookies stuffed with figs, chocolate, and chopped almonds and dipped in honey, which probably originated from the Arab influence on the cuisine of Sicily.

Chocolate Meatball Cookies
Makes 24. Prep time: 40 minutes.

5 cups flour
1 cup sugar
1½ teaspoons baking powder
3 tablespoons cocoa
½ cup margarine
1 cup milk
1½ teaspoons allspice
1½ teaspoons cinnamon
1 teaspoon nutmeg
1 cup chopped walnuts

Reserve one cup of flour; sift remaining dry ingredients together. Cut in chunks of the margarine. Add milk and nuts. Knead in enough of the reserved flour to make a soft dough.

Pinch off meatball-sized pieces; roll into a ball. Place on greased cookie sheet and bake at 350° for 20 minutes or until cookies are soft inside but medium hard on the outside. Cool enough to handle before frosting.

Frosting:

2½ cups extra-fine sugar
½ tablespoon orange juice
1 tablespoon margarine
Milk, as needed

Combine all ingredients and add milk to make a medium-thick consistency. Roll cookies in frosting. Let cool on a baking sheet and serve.

Nonna Grace's Sicilian Ricotta Cheesecake
Serves 8-10. Prep time: 60 minutes.

6 eggs
1 cup sugar
1 teaspoon vanilla
½ cup flour
3 pounds fresh ricotta
½ cup bittersweet chocolate chips
Juice of 1 orange
Zest of 1 orange

Preheat oven to 350°.

In a bowl, mix egg, sugar, and vanilla. Add orange juice, zest, and chocolate chips; then add the flour and mix well. Fold in the ricotta cheese.

Spray a 9" or 10" spring form pan with nonstick spray. Pour in the batter. Bake the cake for 60 minutes and let cool on the rack for about 40 minutes. Place in refrigerator, or serve right away. Garnish with fresh strawberries and a dusting of confectioners' sugar.

How to Eat Biscotti

Traditionally, biscotti, twice-baked cookies, were dipped in *Vin Santo* (holy wine) and served as a dessert. *Vin Santo* wine, made from the white grape varieties trebbiano and malvasia, is said to have originated in Prato, Italy, in the Tuscan region. Biscotti are also known as *cantuccini*, the name most commonly used in Tuscany. Most recipes are made using almonds, but now hazelnuts, pistachios, and other hard nuts are used.

I make a few hundred of my Double Chocolate Espresso Almond or Hazelnut Biscotti over the holidays and give some out as gifts to friends. And instead of having "an apple a day," I have "biscotti a day," and I always have a cappuccino or a fresh-pulled espresso around to dip it into. Pure bliss!

Double Chocolate Espresso Hazelnut or Almond Biscotti
Makes 30-40 small cookies. Prep time: 60 minutes.

¾ to 1 cup hazelnuts or almonds
¾ to 1 cup bittersweet chocolate chips
½ cup melted butter
¾ cup sugar
2 eggs
2 teaspoons vanilla
2 cups unbleached all-purpose flour
1½ teaspoons baking powder
¼ teaspoon salt
¼ cup fresh brewed espresso, brought to room temperature; or
    2 tablespoon of espresso powder.

Bake nuts in 350° oven until toasted. Wrap in towel and remove the skins. Grind nuts and chocolate in seed grinder, or food processor, reserving a handful of each. Set aside.

Cream melted butter, sugar, and eggs in a bowl. Add cooled espresso and vanilla.

Combine flour, baking powder, and salt in another large bowl; mix, then add to cream mixture. Blend well. Fold in reserved nuts and ground chocolate. Add dry espresso powder. Mix dough with hands or in a food processor. Divide dough in half and form into two 14" long rolls. Place 2 -12" rolls on oiled sheet pan about 2" apart.

Bake in 350° oven for 30 minutes or until brown. Let cool on rack or in the refrigerator.

Cut ¼" slices at a 40° angle and place in an upright position back on the cookie tray; return to oven for another 15 to 20 minutes. Let cool. Store in an airtight container until served.

Frutta di Modena
Serves 8. Prep time: 30 minutes.

3 cups fresh strawberries
1 cup white grapes
1 cup red grapes
2 vanilla beans
½ cup balsamic vinegar
¼ cup sugar
5 fresh mint leaves

Wash and remove stems from strawberries; cut them in half. Place in a bowl and add the sugar; macerate for 5 to 10 minutes, then mix well.

In a small sauce pan, heat the balsamic vinegar and vanilla bean for 5 minutes. Remove the vanilla bean and let cool.

Wash and prep the grapes.

Place all the above in a large bowl with a lid. Add the mint, stir, and refrigerate for an hour or more—the longer, the better. Serve in fruit cups.

Ricotta Cheese Tarts with Marsala Wine and Raisins
Serves 22-24. Prep time: 30 minutes.

17.3 ounce pack of ready-rolled puff pastry, thawed
1 cup ricotta cheese
1 egg, plus 2 egg yolks
4 tablespoons sugar
2 tablespoons marsala
2 lemons, zested
⅓ cup golden raisins
2 teaspoons pure vanilla extract

Preheat the oven to 375°.

Cut pastry into 3½" rounds and place in cups of a muffin tin. Set the tray aside for 20 minutes.

Put the ricotta cheese in a bowl and add the egg, extra yolks, sugar, Marsala, and lemon zest. Whisk until smooth, then stir in the raisins. Spoon the mixture into the muffin pans.

Bake the tarts for about 20 minutes or until the filling has risen in each and the pastry is crisp and golden. Cool the tarts slightly before easing each one out with a small spatula. Serve warm, dusted with confectioners' sugar.

Granita di Pesci – **Peach Granita**
Serves 4. Prep time: 60 minutes.

2 cups water
1 pound ripe peaches or mangos, unpeeled
⅓ cup sugar
2 tablespoons fresh lemon juice
1 drop vanilla extract
Mint leaves for garnish

Bring water to a boil in medium saucepan. Add fruit and sugar and simmer gently for 30 minutes. Cool, then strain through a sieve, keeping as much pulp as possible. Add lemon juice and vanilla extract.

Freeze for about an hour, scraping the ice crystals that form around the edges into the center every 10 minutes. Mixture should be even, with a grainy consistency. Scoop granita into chilled serving glasses and garnish with mint leaves.

Italian Lemon Sherbet-Stuffed Lemons
Serves 6. Prep time: 40 minutes.

12 medium lemons, tops cut off and scooped out
1 cup fresh whipping cream
1 cup plain yogurt
¾ cup sugar
2 lemons, juiced
3 teaspoons grated lemon zest

In a medium bowl, combine whipping cream and sugar. Whip with a hand mixer on high speed. Fold in lemon juice, yogurt, and lemon zest. On a sheet pan with edges, spread out the liquid as evenly as possible. Place in the freezer for one hour, stirring after 30 minutes. For a courser consistency, use the tines of a fork to stir.

Fill each lemon with sherbet up to the top. Cover with the lemon lid and wrap in plastic wrap until ready to serve. If serving on a plate, cut the bottom of each lemon off so that the lemon can stand upright on the plate. Serve with a mint leave and a chilled glass of limoncello.

Chocolate Amore Torte

Makes 1 torte that serves 12. Prep time: 60 minutes.

½ cup pecans
½ cup walnuts
½ cup brown sugar
¼ teaspoon cinnamon
4 ounces unsalted butter, melted
6 ounces unsalted butter, softened
24 ounces dark Belgian chocolate
¼ cup sugar
6 egg whites, separated
½ cup heavy cream
1 teaspoon vanilla
½ cup espresso coffee, brought to room temperature
1 pint whipping cream
12 mint sprigs
Fresh raspberries for garnish

In a food processor, pulse the walnuts and pecans with the brown sugar, cinnamon, and melted 4 ounces of butter. Press into a 10" nonstick, spring-form pan. Over a bain-marie, whisk the egg yolks and sugar until creamy. Set aside. In a glass bowl with a hand blender, mix the egg whites until soft peaks form.

Over another bain-marie, melt the chocolate and 6 ounces unsalted butter until creamy. Lower the heat and be careful not to over-heat the chocolate. Add the espresso and the vanilla, stirring to mix well.

Whip one cup of the heavy cream and fold into the chocolate. Add the creamy egg yolks, then slowly fold in the egg whites and whipped cream. Keep folding until mixed well.

Pour chocolate mix into the 10" spring form pan, covering the nut crust.

Freeze until ready to serve. Thaw about 1 hour before serving. Cut into 12 slices. If desired, top with a dollop of fresh whipped cream and garnish with a mint sprig and fresh raspberries.

Italian Plum Torte
Makes a 10" Torte. Prep time: 60 minutes.

2 cups pastry flour
¾ cup finely chopped walnuts
¾ cup light brown sugar, lightly packed
12 tablespoons (1½ stick) cold, unsalted butter, diced
1 egg yolk
2 pounds ripe Italian plums, pitted and quartered lengthwise

Preheat oven to 400°.

Combine flour, nuts, and sugar in a large bowl. Add butter and egg yolk and mix by hand or blender until crumbly. Press 1½ cups of the crumb mixture into an even layer in the bottom of a spring form tart pan.

Arrange plums on top of crumb mixture skin side down. Form a flower pattern with the plum slices starting from the outside and working inward.

Sprinkle the rest of the crumb mixture over the top of the plums and bake for 40 to 50 minutes or until browned. Let cool for 10 minutes and serve with vanilla ice cream or fresh whipped cream.

Grilled Peaches with Amaretti Cream Filling
Serves 10. Prep time: 30 minutes.

5 firm but ripe peaches, peeled and halved
16 ounces almond biscotti
2 large egg yolks
7 tablespoons brown sugar
6 tablespoons lemon juice
3 tablespoons unsalted butter
1 cup chilled whipping cream
Amaretto di Saronno almond liqueur

Remove pits from peaches so that there is a small cavity in each half to fill with the amaretti filling and cream.

Combine 6 tablespoons sugar, lemon juice, and butter in a small saucepan. Add a few tablespoons of Amaretto. Bring to a boil over medium heat, stirring until the sugar dissolves and the butter melts.

Soak the peaches in this syrup, the longer the better, but at least 5 minutes. Grill the peach halves on a medium grill until a little soft but still firm. Alternatively, bake peach halves in a 375° oven.

In a food processor or blender, mix almond biscotti and yolk into purée. Mound filling into peaches. Put peaches on a sheet pan and broil until filling is toasted.

Whip cream with Amaretto liqueur and 1 tablespoon sugar in medium bowl until soft peaks form.

Top each peach with the whipped cream and serve in dessert bowls or long stemmed glasses.

Flaming Bananas Amaretti – An Italian-Style Bananas Foster
Serves 6. Prep time: 20 minutes.

6 ripe bananas, cut into quarters
6 amaretti cookies or small almond biscotti
¼ cup butter (½ stick)
6 tablespoons packed brown sugar
¼ cup orange juice (fresh-squeezed if available)
3 ounces Amaretti di Saronno (almond-flavored liqueur) or dark rum
1 teaspoon cinnamon
2 pints vanilla gelato or French vanilla ice cream
½ cup melted chocolate or chocolate syrup

In a sauté pan or heated 12" cast-iron skillet, melt butter over high heat until it's smoking. Add brown sugar and stir well to make a caramel-like sauce. Do this quickly so the butter doesn't burn.

Peel bananas and cut lengthwise. Add to the sauté pan and cook for a minute or so on both sides. Add liqueur or rum and flame for 30 seconds; then pour orange juice over the top to stop the flame.

Give the bananas a good bath with the sauce. Place on plate and pour remaining sauce over them. Top with a few shakes of cinnamon, and serve with a large scoop of vanilla gelato or ice cream and a drizzle of chocolate sauce. Add the amaretti cookie or biscotti to each dish.

Panna Cotta
Makes 4 small ramekins. Prep time: 40 minutes.

½ cup heavy cream
1 cup half-and-half
1 packet unflavored gelatin
1 teaspoon vanilla extract
½ teaspoon lemon peel
2 tablespoons water, at room temperature
2 tablespoons granulated sugar
Chocolate sauce
Butterscotch

Place water in a small bowl and add the gelatin; set aside to soften. In a small saucepan, combine the heavy cream, half-and-half, lemon zest, and sugar. Bring to a simmer over medium heat. Turn off the heat and add the gelatin mixture, making sure there are no lumps and it is dissolved well.

Whisk for a couple of minutes until the gelatin melts. Strain the mixture with a metal strainer or chinois, then add the vanilla extract and stir.

Divide the mixture between four small ramekins or three large ones. Cover and refrigerate for four hours or overnight.

When ready to serve, gently loosen the Panna Cotta from the ramekin with a small knife and turn upside down on the presentation plate. Drizzle with chocolate sauce or butterscotch sauce, and garnish with a fresh strawberry. Dust with confectioners' sugar and serve.

Fresh raspberries, blueberries, and/or blackberries can also be used.

Ricotta Puffs with Raspberry Sauce and Confectioners' Sugar
Makes 20 puffs. Prep time: 60 minutes.

3 eggs
1 pound fresh ricotta
3 tablespoons sugar
4 teaspoons baking powder
1 cup flour
½ teaspoon salt
1 teaspoon vanilla
Vegetable oil or grape seed oil for frying
1 cup fresh raspberry purée
Confectioners' sugar

Beat eggs in a bowl until fluffy. Add sugar, vanilla, salt, baking powder, and flour; mix well. Stir in ricotta until well blended. Let dough stand for one hour.

Fill saucepan with enough oil to cover puffs, at least ½". Heat oil to 350°. Using a tablespoon to measure the size of puffs, drop little balls into oil and fry for 3 minutes, until golden brown.

With a slotted spoon, remove puffs from oil and drain on paper towels. Sprinkle with confectioners' sugar and serve on top of raspberry purée. Dust with confectioners' sugar.

Roasted Bananas, Pecans, and Strawberries over Mascarpone Cream-Dipped Baguette Slices

Serves 4. Prep time: 30 minutes.

1 thin loaf of Italian or French bread, cut into ¼" slices
1 cup banana, cut into rounds and roasted
1 cup fresh strawberries, cut in half
½ cup pecan pieces, roasted
½ cup mint leaves
1 medium orange zested
Confectioners' sugar
Cinnamon
Mascarpone cheese sauce
3½ ounces mascarpone cream
½ cup confectioners' sugar
1 egg yolk
3 tablespoons orange liqueur
¼ cup whipped cream

Using a whisk, combine the mascarpone, egg yolk, orange liqueur, and confectioners' sugar until smooth. Dip the ¼" cut baguettes into the mix. In a heated sauté pan, melt butter, and brown each baguette slice on both sides in the butter.

Arrange bananas, pecans, and strawberries on a baking sheet and place in 350° oven. Bake until roasted, about 15 minutes.

Place some of the mascarpone cheese mix on plates and place two or three baguette slices on top. Top with pecans, bananas, and strawberries; add a dollop or two of fresh whipped cream. Dust with cinnamon and more confectioners' sugar. Garnish with a few mint leaves and orange zest.

Music is a higher revelation than all wisdom and philosophy. Music is the electrical soil in which the spirit lives, thinks and invents. ~Ludwig van Beethoven

My Coffee Obsession

MY LOVE OF coffee started when I saw my grandfather Colombrito sitting at the kitchen table with a large cup of coffee, actually a very dark-roast espresso. Nonna Grace always used a stovetop coffee pot to make it and I still use one just like it to this day. Grandfather proceeded to mix in some milk, sugar, and day-old Italian bread, to make almost a coffee soup. In the Italian movie *Ill Postino* (*The Postman*), one of the scenes of father and son showed Massimo Troisi, one of the main actors, at the table having coffee this same way.

Going back as far as the tenth century and thought to have originated in Ethiopia, coffee spread throughout the world. Some of the earliest findings were in Yemen, an Arab country in Western Asia. Mocha, the coffee mixed with chocolate we all know from our daily trips to our local coffee shops, originated there and was named after the port of Mocha. They were called mocha beans because they were shipped out of this port. They are now commonly referred to as Arabica beans. It is said that coffee became a religious drink because it reduced the need for sleeping. Around 1600 A.D. it was taken to Europe, where it was considered a medicine but became more popular for its stimulating effects.

The first coffee houses are said to have started in the 17th century in Paris. The Italians learned the art of coffee making from travelers who had been to the Ottoman Empire. One of the most famous composers of music, Johann Sebastian Bach (1685-1750) composed his comic opera *Coffee Cantata,* singing the praises of this great stimulating drink, in 1735. It was first performed in Germany, and is about a young, vivacious woman named Aria who loves coffee. Her killjoy father is against her having any kind of caffeinated fun, and tries to ban her from the drink.

"Ah, how sweet coffee tastes; more delicious than a thousand kisses, milder than muscatel wine. Coffee, I have to have coffee, and if someone wanted to pamper me, oh, then bring me coffee as a gift!" Aria sings.

Father and daughter finally reconcile by having a guarantee written into the marriage contract to have only three cups a day. Very good idea!

Coffee makers in Turkey used to wear white gloves while making the coffee and serving it to the royal Ottoman Sultan. That remains a daily ritual even to this day. There is a Turkish saying, "A cup of coffee creates respect for 40 years to the one who offers it." Today, coffee is the second most consumed product in the world (after petroleum)!

Espresso: 8 tablespoons fine-ground Italian coffee and 1½ cups water

Cappuccino (named after the Cappuccines, a holy order of friars whose robes are the same color as the coffee): 2⅔ cups espresso and 1⅓ cups water

Caffè Latte: 2 cups whole milk and 2 cups Italian-roast coffee

Caffè Mocha: Caffè Latte with chocolate powder or syrup added

Iced coffee: Add milk, sugar, and ice cubes to any of the above

Following are some of my favorite recipes that include coffee.

Coffee Granita

Italian Ice, as *granita* is also known, is enjoyed in many countries all over the world, especially during the summer months. Use whatever flavor syrup you enjoy.
Serves 4. Prep time: 30 minutes.

2 cups freshly brewed espresso or dark roast coffee
½ cup sugar
1 teaspoon coffee liqueur (Torani)
½ teaspoon pure vanilla
Sweetened whipped cream

In a saucepan, combine coffee, sugar, vanilla, and coffee liquor. Stir over low heat until sugar is dissolved.

Pour mixture into a 9" x 13' flat sheet pan and put into the freezer for about 1 hour, until it becomes slushy. Rake a fork through the mixture and place back into the freezer. Do this every 30 minutes or so until completely frozen.

Spoon into tall ice cream glasses and top with sweetened whipped cream.

Tiramisu – Pick Me Up

Tiramisu is said to have been created in 1960 in the region of Veneto at the restaurant Le Beccherie, located in Treviso, Italy. This multilayer dessert has been enjoyed all over the world and served up in a number of different ways. Here is a straightforward, simple version that will surely "pick you up."

Serves 6. Prep time: 30 minutes.

1½ cups espresso, cooled
6 egg yolks
3 tablespoons sugar
1 pound mascarpone cheese
3 tablespoons dark rum
24 ladyfingers, from package
½ cup chocolate powder; or, a chunk of bittersweet chocolate for shaving

In a medium bowl, beat egg yolks well with hand mixer. Whisk in sugar until well blended and pale. Add all the mascarpone and beat until very smooth. Add one tablespoon of espresso and blend well.

Combine remaining espresso and rum in a shallow dish and dip both sides of ladyfingers in it. You can also use a small hand sprayer filled with the espresso and rum to spray each ladyfinger.

Place half the ladyfingers in a 13" x 9" baking dish or casserole dish. Spread half of the mascarpone mix over the first layer of ladyfingers; then add another layer of ladyfingers the same way, and spread the rest of the mascarpone mixture over them.

Sprinkle some dark chocolate powder on the dish; cover and refrigerate at least two hours.

Remove from refrigerator and bring to room temperature; shave some bittersweet chocolate on the top if desired.

Dolce con Ricotta e Caffè – Sweets with Ricotta and Coffee
Serves 6. Prep time: 30 minutes.

1¼ pounds whole-milk ricotta
½ cup whole milk
4 tablespoons sugar
¾ cup freshly brewed espresso coffee
5 chocolate or almond biscotti, crumbled
12 chocolate coffee beans for garnish
½ ounce dark rum or amaretto

In a food processor, place the ricotta cheese, milk, sugar, and espresso coffee, and mix until creamy. Add the biscotti and amaretto, and pulse a few more times.

Spoon into small bowls or dessert cups and garnish with a few chocolate coffee beans. You may also choose to put a dollop of fresh whipped cream on top.

Affogato – Drowned
Serves 2. Prep time: 30 minutes.

2 scoops vanilla gelato
2 shots of freshly brewed espresso
2 dollops of fresh whipped cream
1 tablespoons chocolate powder, chocolate shavings, or chocolate espresso beans
2 shots of Kahlua liquor (optional)

In a dessert cup or bowl, place one healthy scoop of vanilla gelato. Pour the freshly brewed espresso over it slowly. If using the liquor, pour it in now. Put a dollop of fresh whipped cream on the top and garnish with chocolate powder chocolate shavings, or chocolate covered espresso beans. Enjoy!

Music gives a soul to the universe, wings to the mind, flight to the imagination and life to everything. ~Plato

Apéritifs and Digestifs ~*Amari*

APÉRITIFS AND DIGESTIFS are alcoholic beverages and are normally served with meals. An apéritif is usually served before the meal to stimulate the appetite. The word comes from the Latin for "to open." Italians prefer bitter apéritifs like Campari and Aperol, which are commonly served with small food like crackers, cheese, or olives.

Digestifs are served after the meal to aid digestion. They contain herbs and spices that have stomach-settling properties. The first digestifs were made by the Greeks and Romans. Apéritifs and digestifs are collectively known as amari. The word refers to "bitterness," which is common to this group of liqueurs. Following are some of my favorite before- and after-dinner drinks.

Campari

Campari was invented in 1860 by Gaspari Campari in Novara, Italy. It was originally colored by carmine dye derived from crushed cochineal insects that gave it a red color. In 2006, Campari stopped using carmine in its production. Campari is flavored with 68 different fruits, herbs, and spices, including quinine, rhubarb, ginseng, and the peel of bitter oranges. These are pounded together to render its distinctive flavor, and then mixed with alcohol and distilled water.

Campari and Orange
Serves 2. Prep time: 10 minutes.

2 parts (1½ ounces/4 cl) Campari
1 part (¾ ounce/2 cl) soda
3 parts (2¼ ounces/ 6 cl) prosecco
Ice
1 orange slice

Pour these together into a short or tall glass with ice and garnish with an orange slice.

Frangelico Tuscan-Mule

Frangelico is based on a 17th century liquor made with hazelnuts and local herbs by Christian monks in the Piedmont Hills of Northern Italy. It has a toasty flavor with hints of vanilla and white chocolate. Try it in a cup of thick hot chocolate. You will absolutely sing its praises.
Serves 2. Prep time: 10 minutes.

1½ ounces Frangelico
4 ounces ginger ale
1 orange slice

Pour beverages into a tall glass and garnish with orange slice.

Homemade Limoncello

This is one of my favorite after-dinner dessert drinks. It is served ice cold. If you can get organic lemons, use them; or, if you know someone from the Amalfi Coast in Italy, maybe they can send you a box of the type of large lemon called Sfusato. Grown on the Amalfi coast, this lemon has a pronounced point on the end of it, also called a nipple. They are very tart and juicy, with very few seeds. Here is a good recipe if you would like to make your own.
Makes two quart-sized bottles. Prep time: 40 minutes.

15 medium lemons with thick skins
2 bottles (750 ml) 100 proof vodka
4 cups sugar
5 cups water

Wash the lemons well with a brush to remove the pesticides if not organic. Dry them with paper towels. Zest with a zester so there is no white pith remaining.

In a one gallon jar, pour in one bottle of vodka and lemon zest as it is zested. Cover jar and let sit at room temperature for 20 days in a cool, dark place. The more it rests the better. The vodka will take on the color of the zest.

In a saucepan, combine sugar and water and cook until thickened, about 5 to 7 minutes. Let syrup cool before adding it to the Limoncello mixture.

Add the second bottle of vodka. Let rest for another 10 to 14 days.

Strain, then bottle, discarding the lemon zest.

Keep in the refrigerator until ready to serve in chilled glasses.

Classic Bellini

The Bellini is said to be invented by Giuseppe Cipriani, the founder of Harry's Bar in Venice, Italy, sometime between 1934 and 1938. He named the drink Bellini because its unique pink color reminded him of a saint's toga in a painting by 15th century Venetian artist, Giovani Bellini.
Serves 12. Prep time: 10 minutes.

2 cups sugar
1 cup water
6 bottles Prosecco
16 ounces frozen peaches
16 ounces frozen strawberries
Fresh raspberries for garnish
1 teaspoon grated orange peel
Orange peel twists for garnish

In a large saucepan over medium heat, stir the sugar into the water until it dissolves to make a simple syrup. Let it cool. In a blender or food processor, purée the peaches and orange peel with ½ cup of the simple syrup. Strain through a cheesecloth or fine strainer into a medium bowl and refrigerate.

In a clean blender, purée the strawberries with ⅓ cup of the simple sugar syrup until smooth. Strain into another bowl.

Pour each of the two purées into clear glass bowls or small pitchers.

For each serving, pour 2 to 4 tablespoons of the desired fruit purée into a champagne flute. Slowly pour the Prosecco into the flute to fill. Stir to blend. Garnish with a twist of orange peel and enjoy!

Prosecco Raspberry Bellini
Serves 8. Prep time: 20 minutes.

20 ounces frozen raspberries in syrup, thawed
12 ounces frozen lemonade concentrate, thawed
Fresh raspberries
Lemon slices
3 bottles (750 ml each) chilled Prosecco

Purée raspberries in blender or food processor until smooth. Strain into 2-cup pitcher. Cover and refrigerate.

Set out lemonade concentrate, raspberry purée, fresh raspberries, and lemon slices with champagne flutes and prosecco. Pour 2 to 4 tablespoons raspberry purée or lemonade concentrate into each flute. Slowly fill the flutes with prosecco. Garnish with fresh raspberries or lemon slices.

Negroni

This drink is named for Count Negroni, who created it in Florence after World War II. Serves 2. Prep time: 10 minutes.

1 ounce Campari
1 ounce sweet vermouth
1 ounce gin
1 slice lemon or orange
Ice

Put ice and liquid ingredients into a cocktail shaker. Shake, then strain into a chilled glass. Garnish with lemon or orange slice.

Do you know that our soul is composed of harmony? ~Leonardo Da Vinci

Olive Oil

HOMER, THE IMMORTAL Greek poet, was right on when he said olive oil is "liquid gold." It is not just used as a food, but there are a number of other uses. The Romans promoted it as an after-bath rub to smooth and soften the skin. (Try it; it works!) They also used it to light lamps.

The Spanish and Portuguese introduced olive oil to the west in the 15th and 16th century, and the Franciscans in the 18th century were growing it in groves in California. The countries in the Mediterranean harvest some of the very best olive oil with their soil and temperate climate.

You will taste the difference from region to region in each olive oil that is produced from that area. I personally like the olive oil from the region of Puglia. Puglia produces about 40% of Italy's olive oil. They have over 60 million olive trees, and some of them are so old they are protected by the government and considered a national treasure. Bold and fruity, Pugliese olive oil has not only great flavor, but also a high vitamin content. It is rich in polyphenols and other healthful nutrients. The dominant olives in Pugliese oils are coratina, provenzale, and ogliarola. Most of Puglia's olive oil goes into the mass-produced oils; however, you can find some great extra virgin olive oil products here in the

States. I personally like the olive oils of Le Sorrelle. Le Sorrelle translates to "the sisters." Anna and Donatella, the owners of this imported oil brand (as well as gluten-free pasta products) are dear friends of mine.

There are over sixty varieties of olives worldwide. The color will be in direct relation to the variety of olive. There are three main stages of color: green, red, and black. The red ripe olive has a sweet, fruity flavor; the green olive is pungent, strong, and bitterly stringent. The taste of the black olive is described as "old."

Different olive growers prefer different types of olives, and different ways of processing them. The quality of the olive oil, they say, depends not on the quality of the olive, but in the way it is processed. The lighter the color, the more refined it is and the more flavor it has. Pure olive oil is great for salads; fine olive oil is excellent for frying. Extra-virgin oil is best for salads. It is full of flavor and has a dark color. Lighter oils are great for massage. (Try it; you might find the perfect mate just by your scent alone!) Some feel that the best olives for processing are those that have been allowed to ripen on the tree.

All olive oil is cold-pressed. This is the first step after picking the olives for processing. There are four ways to cure olives. The Spanish cure involves a lye process, while the Sicilian cure involves water and salt. The Greeks use a dry salt cure. There is also a pure water method of curing. All cures pull the glycoside from the olive; glycoside is the unpalatable, indigestible substance in the olive.

It takes about 200 medium-sized olives to make 5 ounces of extra virgin olive oil. The olive itself is about 50 percent water, 22 percent oil, 19.1 percent sugar, 1.6 percent protein, and 7.3 percent other organic substances. Olives are not fattening—they average only 4 to 5 calories each and contain no cholesterol. Olives naturally contain vitamins B-6, B-12, A, and C, as well as fiber, ash, protein, and many essential minerals needed for a healthy diet.

Some olive folk lore: "A branch over the door keeps out witches and wizards."

Those who wish to sing always find a song. ~Swedish Proverb

Wine and Cheese

For the Wine Connoisseur, *Ah Salute*!

WINE IS CONSIDERED a food by gourmets the world over. There are different varieties to complement any Italian meal; some are even used in the preparation and cooking. Here is a list of some of the most famous regions and their special *vinos*.

Piedmont: Barolo, Barbara, Barbaresco, Freisa, Asti Spumante
Lombardy: Frecciarossa, the rose wines of Lago di Garda
Venice: Santa Maddalena, Santa Giustina, Termeno, Reisling, Teriano (all from the Trentino area), Soave and Valpolicella from the Verona region
Emilia: Lambrusco, Sangiovese
Tuscany: Chianti, Brunello
The Marches: Verdiccio
Umbria: White Orvito
Lazio: Wines of Castelli Romani, and the wine intriguingly named EST! EST! EST!
Abruzzo: Montepulciano
Campania: Gragnano, white Capri, Malvasia

Wine and Cheese

Basilicata: Anglianico del Vulture
Sicily: Etna wines, Moscato from Pantelleria, Corvo di Salaparuta
Sardinia: Vernaccia, Ogliastra, Oliena

I always felt the earth move after having a few sips of my grandfather Lo Russo's "dago red" wine. It must be one of the reasons he lived to be over 85 years old.

There are many Italian wines available in the U.S. And, there are many small vineyards in the U.S. making fantastic wines. I had the pleasure of tasting Gregg Miller's special blend. It just got better as the meal went on. Here is his story:
Wine and food have always been a my passion. I prefer big, bold reds that stand up to bold favors. I make wine in very small batches using ultra-premier fruit from Napa Valley, so I am able to maintain the delicate balance between fruit, oak, and tannins. My wines are aged in French and American new oak for no less than 3½ years. Most of my production is given to friends and family, however a limited amount is available for purchase depending upon the vintage. ~Gregg Miller, Castillo di Cielo Cellars

Cheese Selection Tips

In Florence, Italy, I was treated a wonderful dinner at Enoteca Pinchiorri, one of the most popular *Enotecas* in the city. *Enoteca* is an Italian word derived from the Greek which literally means "wine repository." The word is used to describe a special type of local or regional wine shop. In addition to the seven courses we were served, there was, at the end of the meal, a most enticing and flavorful cheese platter that was served on a slab of Italian marble. It was hard to resist. Some fresh pears topped the platter off, so we had sweet and crunchy taste and texture.

A good rule of thumb for offering this elaborate ending to a fabulous Italian meal is to mix the four categories of cheeses: *firm* (parmigiano-reggiano, manchego, parmesan, grana padano), *soft*: (camembert, goat cheese, Teleggio), *blue* (stilton, gorgonzola, roquefort), and *aged* (cheddar, gouda).

Also, choose cheeses that are made from different types of milk: cow, sheep, and goat. This combination will give your guests a few tasty and textured flavor profiles that will keep them coming back for more. Serve 1 to 2 ounces of each cheese per person. Place them on your serving platter and separate strong from the mild so that your guests can have the fun taste of each. Each cheese should have its own knife. If served after dinner, serve with grapes, dried fruit, fresh or dried figs, toasted nuts, jams, and honey. In the fall season, add some ripe pears.

As long as we live, there is never enough singing. ~Martin Luther

Suggested Songs & Menus

LISTEN TO SAMPLES of the following songs! Go to http://www.SingingChef.com/Audio to hear many of these songs; or, listen to a sample of all of them by going to Amazon.com and searching "Andy LoRusso/music."

That's Amore
Appetizer: Crostini with Gorgonzola, Roasted Peppers, and Balsamic Glaze
Salad: Burrata Cheese and Heirloom Tomatos
Entrée: Turkey Bolognese over Pappardelle
Dessert: Nonna Grace's Sicilian Ricotta Cheesecake

Volare
Appetizer: Crostini with Olive Tapenade
Salad: Sweet Fennel and Orange Salad with Toasted Walnuts in a Honey-Sherry Vinaigrette
Entrée: Chicken Piccata
Side: Roasted Garlic Mashed Potatoes
Side: Seasonal Julienne Veggies
Dessert: Panna Cotta

Arriverderci Roma
Appetizer: Assorted Italian and Greek Olives with Prosciutto-Wrapped Grissini
Salad: Bocconcini Caprese Salad
Entrée: Roman Chicken
Side: Stuffed Artichokes
Dessert: Double Chocolate Hazelnut or Almond Biscotti

Santa Lucia
Appetizer: Grilled Shrimp and Polenta Wedges with Feta Cheese and Roasted Red Pepper Sauce
Salad: Escarole with Walnuts, Anchovies, and Parmesan
Entrée: Grilled Baby Tuna Steaks with Toasted Almond-Basil Pesto
Side: Prosciutto-Wrapped Asparagus
Dessert: Ricotta Tarts

O Sole Mio
Appetizer: Sicilian Caponata on Grilled Crostini
Salad: Tuscan Panzanella Salad
Entrée: Sicilian Roasted Leg of Lamb with Oven-Roasted Potatoes
Side: Garlicky Mushrooms
Dessert: Sicilian Cannoli

Torna a Sorrento
Appetizer: Stuffed Portobello Mushrooms
Salad: Belgium Endive with Goat Cheese and Toasted Walnuts
Entrée: *Braciola alla Marinara* (Stuffed Flank Steaks in Marinara Sauce)
Side: Broccoli Rape
Side: Creamy Mascarpone Cheese Polenta
Dessert: Italian Plum Torte

A Donna e Mobile
Appetizer: Crostini with Caramelized Onions, Roasted Eggplant, and Cracked Green Olives
Salad: Grilled Shrimp, Fennel, and Radicchio with Balsamic Syrup
Entrée: Chicken Marsala
Side: Garlicky Mushrooms
Dessert: Chocolate Amore Torte

Suggested Songs and Menus

Non ti Sorda di Me
Appetizer: Bruschetta with Yellow and Red Tomatoes and Buffalo Mozzarella
Salad: Grilled Eggplant Roulades
Entrée: Grilled Halibut with Saffron-Orange Aioli Sauce in Soft Tortilla
Dessert: Frutta di Modena-

Martha
Appetizer: Firecracker Stuffed Red Bell peppers
Salad: Escarole with Walnuts, Anchovies, and Parmesan
Entrée: Chicken Scaloppini with Lemon and Capers
Side: Roasted Asparagus
Dessert: Ricotta Tarts

Funiculi, Funicula
Appetizer: Deep Fried Ravioli with Marinara Sauce
Salad: Mozzarella alla Caprese Tower with Grilled Eggplant Slices
Entrée: Fusilli Pasta with Walnut Pesto and Cheese
Dessert: Frutta di Modena

Let us go singing as far as we go: the road will be less tedious. ~Virgil

Global Adventures & Recipes

IN EVERY COUNTRY that I've traveled over the last number of years, I've found that most people like going out to eat, but enjoy time with their family and friends most at the home dinner table. No matter what language is spoken by the guest, everyone can relate to food that looks good, tastes good, and creates a good feeling.

MILAN, ITALY

In 2000, we were visiting my grandfather Angelo's niece – my cousin – Anna LoRusso Bellino and her family, in a small town named Origgio that is located outside of Milan. The family moved there from Potenza many years ago to find good jobs near the city. So this is where they made their home.

I had some of the best homemade Italian meals, along with some very strong *vino* that her husband, Luciano, whose family was from Puglia, made in a small still that was out in the back garage. They also had an area closed-in with a tarp, so that even in the cold winter they could grow greens like spinach, chard, basil, parsley, and other herbs, which Anna used in her cooking. She taught me how to make the traditional cavatelli pasta and how to create indentations with four fingers and a small knife that allow the noodles to catch the chunks of sauces beautifully.

Another typical pasta of Basilicata she showed me was made by rolling small, log-shaped dough around a thin iron rod, about 12" in length, creating a hollow pasta that needs to be shaped one at a time. She did this on a wooden board with raised rims that the family brought up from the farm on Potenza many years ago. It was a wonderful sight to see.

Blood oranges, walnuts, and other items were sent to them from the family that was still living and growing on the same farm my grandfather Angelo grew up on in Potenza.

Luciano also had a brick wood-fired oven in the outside basement to make pizza and calzones, and grill lamb, beef, pork, and fresh fish. It was a great visit with the family and our time spent with them will always have a special place in my heart.

Following are some of the dishes that my cousin Anna made for me while I was there.

Orecchiette alla Potentina - Orecchiette with Mozzarella and Meatballs

Orecchiette is a variety of homemade pasta typical of the Apulia region of southern Italy. The name means "little ears" and comes from its shape, which resembles a small ear. Serves 6. Prep time: 30 minutes.

1 pound orecchiette pasta
½ pound lean ground beef
½ pound pork
2 cloves garlic, minced
1 large egg, beaten
1 cup Italian herbed bread crumbs
¼ cup whole milk
3 tablespoons Italian flat-leave parsley, minced
2 tablespoons sea salt
½ teaspoon freshly ground pepper
¼ teaspoon hot chili flakes
2 tablespoons extra virgin olive oil
4 cups chopped San Marzano tomatoes
½ pound fresh or smoked mozzarella
¼ cup Pecorino Romano cheese, grated

Preheat oven to 425°.

In a large glass bowl, mix the beef, pork, eggs, bread crumbs, salt, pepper, milk, and parsley until blended well. Mix with your hands until smooth then roll into small balls.

In a large sauté pan, heat the olive oil and brown the meatballs about 10 minutes. Add the chopped tomatoes and season with salt and pepper to taste. Simmer for about 15 minutes.

Cook the pasta according to directions on the package and drain well, reserving one cup of the cooking water to dilute the sauce. Fold into the pan with the meatballs. Cook for about 2 minutes, until the pasta has absorbed some of the sauce.

Transfer to a terra-cotta dish, top with the cheeses, and bake in the oven for about 15 minutes. Serve and sing!

Cavatelli con Cime di Rapa e Pangrattato – **Pasta with Broccoli Rabe and Breadcrumbs**

Cavatelli are small pasta shells that look like miniature hot dog buns. Cavatelli means "little hollows." They are able to hold within them the flavorful sauces that they are served with.
Serves 4-6. Prep time: 30 minutes.

1 pound cavatelli pasta
2 bunches broccoli rabe, washed, stems removed
¼ cup Italian bread crumbs
2 anchovy fillets, packed in olive oil, drained and chopped well
4 garlic cloves, chopped
2 dried red chili peppers, crushed; or, ½ teaspoon chili flakes
1 teaspoon sea salt
1 tablespoon ground black pepper

In a medium sauté pan, cook bread crumbs over low to medium heat, until brown, about 3 minutes, and transfer to a plate. In the same sauté pan, heat the olive oil, anchovies, garlic, and chili peppers until the anchovies are soft, about two minutes. Do not burn the garlic.

In a pot with boiling water, add salt, cavatelli, and broccoli rabe that has been steamed to a soft consistency, and stir. Cook until the cavatelli are *al dente*, about 10 minutes. Drain, reserving one cup of pasta water.

On a serving platter, toss the cavatelli and broccoli rape with the infused oil and ladle some of the pasta water over it all to create a sauce like dish. Adjust the seasoning and top with the toasted bread crumbs.

Minestra di Pasta e Ceci – Spicy Pasta and Chickpea Soup

Minestra comes from the Italian word *minestrare* – to serve – and refers to a hearty vegetable soup that includes some type of small pasta. My father used to make this from time to time and it served us well. Add a freshly baked loaf of Italian bread with olive oil and you have a full meal.
Serves 6. Prep time: 30 minutes.

4 cups chicken stock or water
¼ pound tagliatelle pasta, cut into 3" lengths
2 cups cooked (or a 15 ounce can) chickpeas, drained
3 tablespoons extra virgin olive oil
2 garlic cloves, pealed
¼ teaspoon cayenne pepper or red pepper flakes
1 tablespoons Italian flat-leave parsley
12 basil leaves, torn
Sea salt
2 plum tomatoes, peeled, seeded, and diced
¼ cup Pecorino Romano cheese, freshly grated

Place chickpeas in a food processor, reserving ¼ cup. Pulse and purée. Add olive oil, salt, chicken stock, garlic, cayenne, and parsley and process to a smooth paste.

Transfer to a large pot and add the ¼ cup of reserved chickpeas, basil, and tomatoes. Cook over medium heat for about 30 minutes. Add more water to thin if needed.

Cook the pasta *al dente*. Add to the chick pea mixture, stirring often. Serve hot, topped with the cheese and a drizzle of olive oil.

Blood Oranges with Honey and Cinnamon

Blood oranges originated in Sicily and Spain. Some of the varieties are tarocco, moro, and sanguinello. The blood orange is a natural mutation of the orange. They have a unique flavor profile, being distinctly raspberry-like in addition to the usual citrus notes. Serves 6. Prep time: 30 minutes.

4 medium blood oranges in season
¼ cup light honey
1 cinnamon stick
½ cup orange-flower water or Grand Mariner
½ cup sliced almonds, toasted

Using a small, sharp utility knife, remove the peel and the bitter white pith from the blood oranges. Thinly slice the oranges into rounds and arrange in a shallow bowl.

In a sauté pan over low heat, combine the honey, orange-flower water or Grand Mariner, and cinnamon stick. Stir until the mixture comes to a simmer.

Pour the hot syrup over the oranges. Mix well and let cool to room temperature.

Place three slices on each dessert plate and sprinkle some of the toasted almonds over each. Serve at room temperature.

LONDON AND THE ISLE OF WIGHT

In 1970, one of the largest festivals in the United Kingdom was held in Seaclose Park, Newport, on the Isle of Wight. A small island off the coast of southern England, this charming and quaint isle, which was once the summer home of Queen Victoria, came alive the second weekend of June. Bob Dylan and the Band were some of the very first headliners. An estimated 150,000 to 250,000 attended the first concerts there. Performers like Jefferson Airplane, The Who, Joe Cocker, and Jimmy Hendricks, to name a few, were some of the headliners over the years.

The headliners in 2008 were Sting and The Police. They were flown in by helicopter to due to the sea of people that filled the field. The Kaiser Chiefs, the Sex Pistols, the Sugar Babies, and Iggy Pop and the Stooges, plus many more bands from the UK, were there that year. Over 55,000 people were in attendance. That's the year I was contacted by the festival organizer, John Giddings, to perform under the Big Top tent. It was the first year they added this area to the Festival, and they wanted to showcase it with up-and-coming acts. I had been talking with an agent in London, Richard Smith, about bookings in the UK. He knew John Giddings, and it all came together very nicely for the three of us to come up with a show date for me.

As I walked around the grounds of Seaclose Park, I could feel the presence of some of the greatest rock performers of all time. The field was dry and dusty, with no rain in sight, and was teeming with the energy and anticipation of the 70,000 fans who came for the shows over the next three exciting days.

My agent in the UK knew a terrific up-and-coming chef, Tim Salt, who was living and working on the Isle of Wight, and contracted him to be my Sous-chef. We ended up using one of the kitchens that he worked in on the Isle of Wight to prep the recipes I cooked for my two shows.

The caterers that provided food for the acts and performers in the Big Top tent went out of their way to provide the very best of every kind of food you could think of, using fresh ingredients that were brought in by the ferry or grown locally. There were plenty of alcoholic beverages for those who had backstage passes, and boy! Those folks from the UK really liked to drink.

I, my agent from London, and his wife all stayed at a charming bed and breakfast that was a former convent. Our rooms came with a fabulous English breakfast fit for any Englishman and touring guest. Each morning we had bacon, sunny-side-up or scrambled eggs, sausages, fried mushrooms, grilled bread, hash browns, white toast with homemade orange marmalade, baked beans, black pudding, sliced tomatoes, and of course, English tea. There was also a jar of Vegemite, a thick, black Australian food made from Brewer's yeast extract with varying vegetables and spice additives that will make anyone's face pucker up. It's an acquired taste for sure.

During my two 45-minute shows, one each day under the Big Top, I was welcomed with open arms – and stomachs – as I sang a few of the Italian songs that are on my *That's Amore* CD. The audience of close to 2,000 people was invited to sing along. I also debuted one of my original songs, called *Foodwraps* because I rap about food and the fun of preparing it. I had one of the security guards pick at least five men from the crowd to join me and dance a choreographed routine to my original songs *Grillin' and Chillin'* and *Cooking with the Family* (see links on my website, www.singingchef.com). It was a hoot and everyone had a great time and a good laugh.

The recipes I prepared for my shows were Orange and Fennel Salad, made with baby organic arugula, toasted walnuts, and sweet orange slices and dressed with a honey-sherry vinegar; Nonna Grace's Ricotta Cheesecake; Nonna Grace's Polenta; Bruschetta with Gorgonzola Cheese, Roasted Red Peppers, Kalamata Olives, and Roasted Garlic; and Banana Amaretto – my take on the classic Bananas Foster – with chopped bananas swirled in brown sugar and butter, flamed with amaretto instead of brandy, then topped with vanilla ice cream. Delish!

Here are a few classic items that are British staples.

Fish and Chips, London Style
Serves 4. Prep time: 30 minutes.

1½ pounds cod fillets
1 egg
1 quart vegetable oil for frying
4 large russet potatoes, peeled and cut into strips
1 cup all-purpose flour
1 teaspoon baking powder
Salt and freshly ground black pepper

In a medium bowl of cold water, place peeled potatoes. In a medium mixing bowl, mix together baking powder, salt, and pepper. Stir in the milk and egg and stir until the mixture is smooth. Let batter sit for 20 minutes.

In a large skillet, heat the oil to 350°. Fry the potatoes in the hot oil until they are tender. Drain, season with salt and set aside.

Dredge the fish in the batter one piece at a time and slowly place them in the hot oil. Fry until the fish is golden brown. If necessary, increase the heat to maintain the 350° temperature.

For added crispness, fry the potato again for about 2 minutes. Season with salt and serve with the fried fish. Sprinkle with vinegar if so desired.

Classic Mushy Peas
Serves 4. Prep time: 30 minutes.

10 ounce package of frozen peas
¼ cup heavy cream
1 tablespoon butter
Sea salt and freshly ground pepper to taste

In a saucepan of salted boiling water, add frozen peas and cook until tender. Drain and put into a food processor or blender.

Add cream butter, salt, and pepper. Process until thin but still with some small pieces of peas for texture. Adjust seasoning as desired. Great served with Fish and Chips!

Bangers and Mash (Sausages and Potatoes) with Onion Gravy
Serve 8. Prep time: 60 minutes.

8 sweet or hot sausages
2 medium onions, sliced into rounds
½ teaspoon spicy mustard
20 ounces beef or chicken stock
3 tablespoons unsalted butter, softened
Black pepper
2 tablespoons unbleached flour

For the Mash
2 pounds white potatoes, peeled and chopped into equally-sized pieces
1¾ ounces butter
3½ ounces whole milk
10 ounces frozen peas
Mixed dried herbs

Preheat oven to 400°.

Place sausages in a roasting pan and cook in oven for about 10 minutes until done. Add the sliced onions to the roasting pan.

In a mixing bowl, combine the mixed herbs, mustard, and stock. Pour over the sausages and onions. Return to the oven and cook for about 20 minutes, or until the onion gravy is thickened.

In a pot of boiling water, cook the potatoes until tender, then drain, season, and mash with a potato masher. Add the milk with the melted butter to the mashed potatoes and mix until smooth. Set aside.

Cook peas by steaming 2-3 minutes; drain and set aside.

For the gravy, mix the butter and flour and stir well. Whisk until smooth over low heat in another saucepan. Pour over the sausages and onions, and serve.

ISTANBUL, TURKEY - "CROSSROADS OF THE WORLD"

The Singing Chef Show® at the Longtable Restaurant in the posh Sofa Hotel in downtown Istanbul, Turkey in June 2010 was a smash hit. Over 200 people attended each night, and not only ate delicious Mediterranean food cooked by the well-known stellar chefs Gazi and Bilal, but sang along to all the Italian songs I sang.

I was booked by Capa-Marka Entertainment Productions, which oversees four exclusive restaurants in Istanbul owned and operated by one of Turkey's top restaurateurs and show promoters, Izzet Capa. Other celebrities who have been invited there include Bo Derek, Mariel Hemingway, Steve Guttenberg, and a host of world-famous DJs. It is the place to see and be seen. Thank you to the people of Istanbul for welcoming me with open hearts and making me feel right at home. Hope to see you all again real soon.

I was pleasantly surprised that almost all the people who attended my shows at the Longtable were familiar with the American icon Dean Martin, and knew all the words to the songs I sang. The top chefs who assisted me gave me the best inspiration they could have, as they also loved everything Italian and shared their special recipes.

The Turkish breakfast called *kahvalti* (which means "before coffee") that I woke up to each morning was a sight to see and stellar to eat. Some of the items from the Turkish breakfast buffet at the hotel that I thoroughly enjoyed incude dried apricots, freshly-made yogurt, stuffed grape leaves, cucumbers, pita breads and crusty French baguettes, black and green olives, salami and other cured meats, feta cheese, light honey, red and green grapes, flat bread crackers, hard-boiled and soft-boiled eggs, cooked ham, extra virgin olive oil, Turkish black teas, and the traditional omelet called *menemen*.

While walking on the streets in Istanbul with my chaperone Anji Harvard, who was from Mongolia and worked for the agency Capa-Marka that booked me, I had the opportunity to have freshly squeezed pomegranate juice. It was very refreshing and a wonderful taste treat. In fact, it tasted so good that I couldn't wait to have another. I vowed to have this fruit as a regular part of my diet when I got back home.

Here is one of the favorite breakfast items of Turks.

Menemen
Serves 4. Prep time: 30 minutes.

4 large eggs
1 Cubanelle pepper or green bell pepper, sliced thinly
3 ripe tomatoes, peeled and diced
2 tablespoons extra virgin olive oil
Salt and black pepper

In a sauté pan, add the olive oil over medium heat. Add the tomatoes and cover to allow the tomato juices to stay in the pan. Cook about five minutes, or until they are soft. Add the green pepper and cook for a few more minutes until soft.

In a medium bowl, beat the eggs and season with salt and black pepper. Slowly pour the beaten eggs in the pan with the tomatoes and peppers, coating them all. With the heat on low, cover for a few more minutes until the eggs become soft. Enjoy with some fresh pita or crusty French bread.

Turkish Red Lentil Soup with Fresh Mint
Serves 6. Prep time: 40 minutes.

¼ cup white long or short grain rice
2 garlic cloves, minced
½ sweet onion, diced
¼ cup tomatoes, diced
5 cups low-sodium chicken stock
½ cup red lentils
½ cup bulgur
2 tablespoons paprika
3 tablespoons tomato paste
½ teaspoon cayenne pepper
2 tablespoons fresh mint, chopped

Heat olive oil in a large soup pot over high heat. Cook the onion in the oil until it begins to soften. Add the garlic and cook for a few more minutes. Add the diced tomatoes to the onion mixture and cook on low for another 10 minutes.

Pour in the chicken stock, red lentils, bulgur, tomato paste, paprika, cayenne pepper, and mint into the tomato mixture. Season with salt and black pepper. Bring to a boil, reduce heat to medium-low and simmer until the lentils and rice are cooked through, about 30 minutes.

Pour soup into a blender or food processor to no more than half full. Give a few quick pulses so the soup can loosen, and then on puree. Puree in batches until smooth. Pour into soup bowls and garnish with fresh mint leaves.

Baby Arugula Salad with Toasted Pecans and Pomegranate
Serves 8. Prep time: 30 minutes.

2 medium bunches baby arugula
¼ cup pecans, coarsely chopped and candied
1½ teaspoons rice wine vinegar
6 tablespoons extra virgin olive oil
Seeds from 1 large pomegranate, deseeded (½ cup)
Sea salt and freshly ground black pepper
Candied Pecans
1 cup white or brown sugar
1 teaspoon sea salt
1 teaspoon ground cinnamon
1 egg white
1 pound pecan halves

Preheat oven to 250°.

Mix sugar, cinnamon, and salt in a small bowl. Whisk egg white and water together in a separate bowl until frothy. Toss pecans in the egg white mixture. then the sugar cinnamon until well coated. Place pecans on a baking sheet and place in the oven until evenly browned, about 1 hour.

In a medium wooden bowl, whisk vinegar, salt, and pepper; slowly add the olive oil until emulsified. Toss arugula with the vinaigrette to coat, then add the candied pecans and pomegranate seeds. Toss again and serve.

THE GILROY GARLIC FESTIVAL, GILROY CALIFORNIA

The Gilroy Garlic Festival, founded by Dr. Rudy Melone in 1978 and held during the garlic harvest, has become one of the go-to festivals of the year in central California. The area 30 miles south of San Jose has a very strong Italian heritage. Dr. Melone coupled with one of the largest garlic ranch shippers in the world, Don Christopher, to make this festival everything garlic.

Allium Sativum, or garlic, is used in many countries to flavor foods, and in some countries is used as a medicine. The nickname "Stinken' Rose" was given to this wondrous bulb. If you roast garlic, it becomes sweeter and easy to spread on bread. This is one of my favorite ways to prepare it.

Garlic has been around for over 7000 years. It's native to central Asia and has long been a staple of the Mediterranean diet. It produces heat in the body, and some cultures say it is a sexual stimulant. As of 2013, China was the largest producer of garlic.

I remember an experience after one of my shows. A young girl came up to the stage, accompanied by her father, and gave me a gift of a small cake cone with garlic ice cream, very concentrated in flavor. I was in for a real experience. It was cool and wet and somewhat sweet. After an hour or so, my body temperature started to rise. My heart rate went up and sweat poured out of me as if I was in the Sahara Desert. Garlic produces heat in the system and this was like eating a whole bulb. Wow! I'll always remember my first garlic ice cream cone.

Here are a few of the recipes that I prepared during the few years that I performing there.

Note that eating some fresh parsley after ingesting garlic will help to freshen the breath. Good advice!

Roasted Garlic, Spinach, Ricotta, Artichoke Gondola Bread
Serves 6. Prep time: 40 minutes.

12 garlic cloves or 2 medium bulbs of roasted garlic
1 cup fresh whole-milk ricotta cheese
1 can artichoke hearts packed in water
1 bunch spinach, sautéed
½ cup Kalamata olives, pitted
1 French or Italian soft baguette
1 cup asiago cheese, ½ cup of it shaved
Kosher salt and black pepper
½ cup extra virgin olive oil
1 bunch of flat-leaf parsley
2 teaspoons red pepper flakes

Preheat oven to 400°.

On a baking sheet, place garlic cloves; or, if using the full bulbs, cut the tops off. Drizzle with olive oil. Add salt and cover with aluminum foil. Roast for about 30 minutes until the garlic is soft and you can squeeze it out of the shell.

Sauté the spinach in olive oil and drain.

Put the roasted garlic, parsley, olives, artichoke hearts, spinach, and ricotta in a food processor and pulse until mixed well. Season with salt, pepper, and red pepper flakes.

Cut the loaf of bread in half lengthwise and scoop out the inside to make a well. Brush with olive oil and fill the well with the ricotta cheese mixture. Shave the asiago cheese over the top of each loaf and place on the baking sheet. Place in a 350° oven and bake for 20 minutes, or until the cheese melts and the bread is golden brown. Let cool and cut into ¼" pieces. Garnish with chopped parsley and serve.

Spicy Garlic Shrimp on Skewers
Serves 6. Prep time: 30 minutes.

1½ pounds medium shrimp, peeled and deveined
8 tablespoons (one stick) unsalted butter, cut into slices
6 cloves garlic, minced
½ cup chicken stock
2 lemons, juiced and zested
2 tablespoons red pepper flakes
3 tablespoons Italian flat-leaf parsley, chopped
Salt and black pepper
6 metal or wooden skewers (If using wooden skewers, soak in water for a few minutes.)

In a large skillet over medium-high heat, melt two tablespoons of the butter. Add the shrimp and cook for about 2 minutes; then add red pepper flakes, salt, and pepper to taste. Cook until shrimp are pink. Remove shrimp to a plate.

In the skillet, deglaze with some chicken stock and add the minced garlic, lemon juice, and zest. Stir well.

Return the shrimp to the skillet and toss for 1 minute. Remove the shrimp and thread three of them onto each skewer.

Heat a gas grill or stove top grill pan to medium heat and place the skewered shrimp on it for 2 minutes on each side. Place each skewer on a plate and garnish with the parsley.

THE CALGARY STAMPEDE, CALGARY, CANADA – "THE GREATEST OUTDOOR SHOW ON EARTH"

Every July, over a million visitors get dressed in their best Western wear and descend upon the beautiful city of Calgary in Canada. For two weeks out of the year, Calgary turns into a real cowtown. The first fair was held back in 1886, and in 1912 American promoter Guy Weadick organized the first rodeo and festival known as the Stampede. It became an annual event when he merged with the Calgary Industrial Exhibition to create what it is now one of the world's richest rodeos and Canada's largest festival.

As I arrived at the airport on my adventure to the Stampede, I was greeted by a committee of women who welcomed me with big hugs, some Calgary lapel pins, and an extra-large Stetson cowboy hat. I already had my western boots shined up and on my feet; but I found out, the locals can tell you're a tenderfoot if your boots are not all scuffed up or muddy.

The ladies took me to my hotel so I could freshen up before dinner. I stayed right in the heart of downtown, at the famous Palliser Hotel. One of the oldest and most luxurious properties now owned by the Fairmount Hotel chain, it was originally built by the Canadian Pacific Railway. I washed up and changed my clothes before I was taken to lunch at Buzzard's Restaurant and Bar, an eatery near the hotel that had great atmosphere. Leather boots, saddles, and bridles hung on the walls with lots of western paraphernalia.

On the menu were some good old cowboy dishes especially for Stampede week, like corn on the cob, roast beef with brown gravy, mashed potatoes, and corn bread. One item on the menu that intrigued me was called Prairie Oysters, also known in the United States as Rocky Mountain Oysters. I was encouraged by my hosts to try them; they insisted I would like them.

I was given a plate with a few chopped walnuts scattered around and some strange looking items that reminded me of large diver scallops. They were pounded, breaded, and deep-fried. I proceeded to eat them; they were a bit chewy but flavorful. Afterwards, I found out that what I had eaten were bull testicles. My hosts sure welcomed me in true Calgary Stampede style and I will never forget this culinary experience.

Over the next two days, I performed two 45-minute shows with food sampling on the cooking stage and had everyone sing along with my music. Giddy up! Here are a few samples of the food that I enjoyed eating during my time in Calgary, Canada, and a few of the unique recipes that you may want to try at home.

Lobster Mac and Cheese

Macaroni and cheese is the ultimate comfort food. Almost everybody I know grew up with some version of this tasty dish. The first recipes of it go back to the late 13th century in southern Italy. For our American version, we have the story of Thomas Jefferson bringing back a pasta machine from Italy, and having macaroni with parmesan cheese served in his home by his hostess Mary.

This version has been updated with not only some savory cheeses, but also that favorite crustacean of the sea, lobster.
Serves 8. Prep time: 40 minutes.

A 2 pound lobster, split
16 ounces elbow macaroni
3 tablespoons unsalted butter
1 small onion, diced
2 cloves garlic, minced
1 small shallot, chopped
10 black peppercorns
2 cup whole milk
½ cup all-purpose flour
1 pound shredded gruyere cheese
3 cups shredded cheddar cheese
1 cup grated Romano or pecorino cheese
½ cup Panko bread crumbs
Sea salt and black pepper to taste

Preheat the oven to 350°.

In a large pot of boiling, salted water, cook the macaroni until still firm to taste. Drain, reserving 2 cups of the pasta water. Rinse with cold water and put into a bowl.

In the same pot, return the reserved pasta water and place the lobster halves into the pot cut-side up. Add more water if needed. Steam just until the meat firms and turns pink, about 3 minutes.

Remove the lobster and let cool for a few minutes, then remove the meat and cut into bite-sized pieces. Reserve the shells.

In a saucepan over medium heat, melt the butter and stir in the onion until it has softened and turns translucent, about 5 minutes. Put into a small bowl and set aside.

Place the reserved lobster shells, shallots, garlic, peppercorns, and milk into the same saucepan. Bring to a simmer over medium heat and cook for 20 minutes.

In another saucepan over medium heat, whisk the flour and stir until the mixture becomes paste-like and light golden brown, about 10 minutes. Strain the milk through a mesh sieve. Gradually whisk the milk and flour mixture, and bring to a simmer over medium heat. Cook and stir until the mixture is smooth and thick, about 10 to 15 minutes.

Stir the cheeses into the thickened milk until melted and smooth. Season to taste with salt and pepper, then stir in the reserved lobster, onions, and macaroni. Pour the lobster macaroni into a 4-quart casserole dish and smooth out the top. Sprinkle evenly with Panko crumbs.

Bake in the pre-heated 350° oven until the sauce is bubbly and the top is golden brown.

Prairie Oysters (also known as Rocky Mountain Oysters)

Eating testicles of healthy, castrated males dates back to the Roman times, when it was believed to be an aphrodisiac. It is still considered so this present day in Asia. Today, ranchers castrate bulls to maintain the herds. Some say the testicles taste like liver or chicken. Give them a try if you dare!
Serves 6. Prep time: 40 minutes.

2 pounds calf testicles (bull testicles are not as tender)
2 cups beer
2 eggs, beaten
1½ cups all-purpose flour
1½ cups yellow corn meal
Salt and freshly ground pepper to taste
2 cups vegetable oil
½ cup hot pepper sauce
1 cup arugula, for garnish

Split the tough skin that covers each muscle with a sharp knife. You can leave them whole or slice them in ¼ to ½" thin ovals. Place them in a large pan with enough beer to cover them. Let sit for two hours.

In a medium bowl, combine, eggs, flour, corn meal, salt, and pepper. Remove testicles from beer and dredge in flour mixture, covering both sides.

In a medium cast iron pan, heat oil to 375°. Deep fry for three minutes, or until golden brown. Drain on paper towels and serve on a plate with the arugula and hot sauce.

CHRISTMAS IN NOVEMBER AT JASPER PARK LODGE IN ALBERTA, CANADA

This Christmas-themed event has been a tradition for the past 29 years at the world-famous Jasper Park Lodge, part of the Fairmont chain of luxury hotels. Celebrating all things Christmas with the talents of many of the top chefs of Canada was an event to remember.

I was invited to this prestigious event back in 1999 and was excited to meet new friends and experience this beautiful part of the Canadian Rockies. Need I say it was cold, bitter cold, especially coming as I was from southern California. Nevertheless, I was ready to give it a go and was layered to the hilt with new winter clothing.

The Jasper Park Lodge was my home for this event, and its drivers picked me up in a limo that thankfully had good heating. We drove though the winding roads covered with snow and ice to our destination. Along the way, I had my first glimpse of bighorn sheep. Beautiful creatures, they were clinging to the side of the mountains like bees on a hive. Very agile and sure-footed, they stood guard as if to approve of the cars below that passed them. They were truly a sight to see.

The Jasper Park Lodge was tucked deep in the mountains, with only one way in and out. It took about an hour to get there, and as I arrived it seemed I had been transported to a winter wonderland. The Loge was decorated with many Christmas ornaments and evergreen trees that were decorated in the lobby. There were glittering glass balls and Christmas stockings hanging from the large fireplaces that warmed the guests as they checked in. A walk down 5th Avenue in New York paled to this display of holiday spirit.

My cabin was very rustic. It was situated at the edge of a lake that was frozen over by a very thick layer of ice. My bedroom had a working stove fireplace that burned wooden logs and heated the whole cabin. It was as cozy as can be.

The Lodge was a short walk away from my little cabin and the path had been recently plowed. A Meet-and-Great dinner was set up that night with a number of stellar chefs from all over Canada, some of whom worked for the Fairmount Hotel chain that the Lodge was a part of. We ate, drank, and shared stories of food, then were given our schedule for the next two days.

On the way back to my cabin, I was stopped dead in my tracks by a large—and I do mean large—female moose, or cow, that was lying on its side blocking the entrance to my door.

When I approached her, she jumped up and stepped two steps towards me, snorted, and then backed off. I looked up by the road, and there, looking over the whole situation, was her mate, a very large bull moose with its huge antlers swinging from side to side. That's when she sprinted off to meet him and they lumbered off in the dark, cold night together. I was happy to get back to my warm cabin alive and will always remember my first encounter with this boreal from the north country. I slept very well that night.

Following are some of the gourmet recipes from my time at the Jasper Lodge. Enjoy the traditional Canadian Christmas fare!

Roasted Butternut Squash Salad with Warm Maple-Walnut Vinaigrette

Serves 6. Prep time: 60 minutes.

4 cups butternut squash, peeled, seeds removed, and chopped
¼ cup olive oil
½ cup dried cranberries
¼ cup red onion, diced
½ cup golden raisins

Rub the squash with olive oil and place on a roasting pan. Roast in a 350° oven for 30 minutes, or until the squash is tender but not mushy. Remove from the oven and let cool.

Place the squash in a medium mixing bowl and add the dried cranberries, red onion, and golden raisins.

Warm Maple-Walnut Vinaigrette

1½ cups sherry wine vinegar
½ cup maple syrup
1 teaspoon lemon juice
¼ cup olive oil
½ cup cardamom
½ teaspoon ginger
¼ cup chopped parsley
½ cup walnuts, toasted and chopped
¼ cup Sortilege maple brandy from Quebec
Salt and pepper to taste

Combine all ingredients except parsley and walnuts in a heavy-bottomed saucepan and bring to a boil for 1 minute, then remove from heat.

Pour the mix over the squash salad and mix thoroughly. Toss in parsley and walnuts and adjust the seasoning if necessary.

This salad can be served hot or cold.

Honey-Basted Grain-Fed Alberta Pork Loin with Fennel and Mustard Crust
Serves 4. Prep time: 60 minutes.

1½ pounds boneless pork loin
¼ cup medium dark honey
2 tablespoons fennel seeds
2 tablespoons mustard seeds
Salt and freshly ground pepper to taste

Trim fat from the pork loin so that only a thin layer remains. Tie the roast with butcher string. Season the roast thoroughly with salt, freshly ground pepper, mustard seeds, and fennel seeds.

In a roasting pan or large fry pan, sear the roast well on both sides and place in a 325° oven for about 45 minutes, until the internal temperature is 145°. Let rest for 15 minutes before carving into thin slices.

Serve with spoon bread with pan gravy and seasonal roasted vegetables.

Bacon-Wrapped Dates Stuffed with Almonds
Serves 12. Prep time: 20 minutes.

24 blanched whole almonds, toasted
24 medium Medjool dates, pitted
8 thin slices bacon, cut into thirds

Toast almonds on a baking sheet at 350° for about 15 minutes.

Stuff an almond inside each date and wrap with bacon.

Sauté the wrapped dates in a fry pan until the bacon is cooked on both sides, about 2 minutes.

Put on small plates and pass around as finger food.

Spoonbread with Bacon and Local Gouda Cheese
Serves 8. Prep time: 30 minutes.

¾ cup cornmeal
½ cup chicken stock
½ cup Gouda cheese, shredded
½ cup butter, softened
2 cloves garlic, minced
1 cup whole milk
4 eggs, separated
3 strips cooked bacon

Spray muffin tin with non-stick spray. In a saucepan, combine cornmeal and water; cook, stirring continually, until mixture boils and thickens. Remove from heat.

Stir in cheese, butter, garlic, and salt and stir until the cheese is melted. Stir in the egg yolks and chopped bacon until well blended.

In a medium bowl, beat the egg whites until stiff peaks form. Fold into the cornmeal mixture. Pour into the muffin tin and bake at 350° for 1 hour, until golden brown and puffy. A knife inserted into the center should come out clean.

Serve hot with the pork loin and roasted vegetables.

Christmas Sugarplums

Makes 36. Prep time: 30 minutes.

½ pound dates (about 1⅔ cups)
½ pound raisins (about 1⅔ cups)
½ cup slivered blanched almonds
½ cup chopped walnuts
⅓ cup crystallized ginger
1 orange peel, finely grated
2 tablespoons brandy or cognac
Granulated sugar

In a food processor, whirl dates and raisins until coarsely chopped. Pour into a large bowl.

Place almonds, walnuts, and ginger into the processor and using an on-off motion, whirl until coarsely chopped.

Stir into the date mixture along with the orange peel and brandy/cognac. Using the hands, mix until blended. Tightly pack into 1" balls. Roll each ball in granulated sugar.

Store in an airtight container, separated by wax paper, in the refrigerator. You can also freeze them for several months.

MILWAUKEE FESTA ITALIANA 40TH ANNIVERSARY, 2017

This is the largest gathering of Italian-Americans and wanna-be Italians in the country. It's held annually at the Henry Maier Festival Park as part of the Summer Fest program. Over 800,000 people attend and enjoy everything Italian.

The festival started back in 1978 as a way to bring together an Italian community torn apart by urban renewal projects. Many Italians whose families had settled in the Milwaukee area longed for the street festivals that took place in the Third Ward during the summertime, and this was like a "coming home" event for all of them. Over 2000 volunteers helped make it happen. Almost every region of Italy is represented on the fairgrounds, and one can not only see the culture from that area, but also taste the fantastic foods that each region has to offer. That alone is worth the price of admission. A large percentage of the money raised goes toward the education of Italian students who qualify for the scholarships available.

One year that I performed on the cooking stage, Mary Ann Esposito, who has a very popular PBS cooking show called *Ciao Italia*, was there also. She was impressed to hear that I sang many of the Italian love songs and arias she grew up listening to in her home.

Following are a few of my favorite dishes from some of the 20 regions of Italy, some of which were represented at the Milwaukee Italian Festival.

Veneto Region - Venice

Venisia, or Venice, is a major seaport. It is made up of a number of islands. I enjoyed visiting this region and some of the numerous attractions, like St. Mark's Basilica, the Grand Canal, and Piazza San Marko, during the millennium. The fresh fish dishes and the small plates of appetizers were some of my favorites. The art and the history of this city, as well as the hand-blown glass on the island of Murano, are fantastic and not to be missed.

Risotto

Risotto is one of the Veneto's most-loved rice dishes. It is well worth the time to prepare this rice that can be prepared in a number of different ways with a number of different ingredients. It all boils down to its preparation and the goodness that comes from the slow cooking of this gem of a grain.

The history of rice in Italy contributes to its widespread use in many regions, and is related to what Spanish cuisine uses for its popular dish, paella. It is said that rice was introduced to Italy and Spain from the Arabs.

Note: Arborio rice is an Italian short grain rice named after the town of Arborio in the Po Valley. It is also grown in Arkansas, California, and Missouri.

Classic Risotto and Portobello Mushrooms
Serves 6. Prep time: 40 minutes.

1½ cups Arborio rice
1 cup sodium-free chicken broth
1 pound portobello mushrooms, thinly sliced
2 medium shallots, diced
¼ cup extra virgin olive oil
½ cup dry white wine
Sea salt and freshly ground black pepper to taste
3 tablespoons finely chopped chives
4 tablespoons butter
⅓ cup freshly grated parmesan or pecorino cheese

In a saucepan, warm chicken broth over low heat.

Warm two tablespoons of olive oil in a separate saucepan over medium-high heat and add the mushrooms. When tender, remove the mushrooms and their liquid and set aside.

In a sauté pan with some olive oil, sauté the shallots for one minute. Add the rice and coat fully with the oil. Cook 2 minutes. When the rice is transparent and a golden color, add the white wine, stirring constantly, until it is all absorbed. Add 1 cup of chicken broth to the rice and cook until it is all absorbed. Continue adding the broth to the rice until all the liquid is absorbed and the rice is *al dente*, about 15 to 20 minutes.

Remove rice from heat, then add butter, chives, and the mushrooms with their liquid. Add salt, pepper, and parmesan. Stir well and serve.

Carpaccio

This dish is said to have been created in a bar in Venice. It is comprised of meat or fish that is thinly sliced then pounded thin and served on a small plate with either capers, lemon, or other sauces like mayonnaise, mustard, cream, or tomato.

Smoked Salmon Carpaccio
Serves 4. Prep time: 20 minutes.

12 ounces smoked salmon
3 tablespoons freshly squeezed lemon juice
1 small red onion, finely chopped
3 teaspoons small capers
¼ cup extra virgin olive oil
Freshly ground black pepper

In a medium bowl, combine olive oil, capers, red onion, lemon juice, and whisk well. Arrange the smoked salmon on small serving plates.

Drizzle the dressing over each plate and grind some black pepper over each.

Emilia-Romagna

Emilia-Romagna, affectionately known as the bread basket of Italy, is one of the wealthiest and most-developed regions in Europe. Its capital is Bologna, which is also the home of the University of Bologna, the oldest university in the world. Known for its fantastic cuisine the world over, it's also the home of my favorite ham, cheese, and vinegar: Prosciutto de Parma, Parmigiano-Reggiano, and Balsamico.

Strawberry and Mascarpone Cheese Crostini with Fresh Mint Leaves
Serves 8. Prep time: 30 minutes.

1 loaf Italian baguette, sliced in ¼ cuts
8 ounces mascarpone cheese
2 teaspoons light honey
1½ cups fresh strawberries, sliced
2 tablespoons good balsamic vinegar
2 tablespoons cinnamon
2 tablespoons raw sugar
¼ cup unsalted butter, melted
8 fresh mint leaves

Preheat oven to 350°.

In a bowl, mix the cinnamon and sugar. Dip each cut of baguette in the melted butter and then into the sugar-cinnamon mixture to cover both sides. Place bread slices on a baking sheet and toast in oven until golden brown. Alternatively, you can toast them in a skillet on medium heat, both sides, until golden brown.

In another bowl, blend mascarpone cheese and honey until well mixed. Spread a dollop of this mixture on each bread slice.

In a bowl, mix the balsamic vinegar with a little bit of sugar. Then add the strawberries and toss until well coated. Top each slice of bread with the strawberries and garnish with fresh mint.

Tuscany

Tuscany, the region in central Italy, is known as the birthplace of the Italian Renaissance. It is recognized not only for its history but also for it world-renowned wines, including Chianti, Vino Nobile de Montepulciano, and Brunello di Montalcino, my favorites. My trip there was fantastic; I got to see some of the prized artifacts from that region in the museums in the capitol city of *Firenze* (Florence). I also tasted some of this region's best-loved dishes.

Ribollita - **Reboiled**

One of the best-known Tuscan soups, this hearty potage made with bread and vegetables is one of my comfort foods. There are many variations, but the main ingredients always include leftover bread, cannellini beans, lacinato kale, cabbage, and vegetables like carrots, beans, Swiss chard, celery, potatoes, and onion.

Ribollita with Grilled Ciabatta Garlic Bread
Serves 6. Prep time: 30 minutes.

15 ounce can diced tomatoes
1 tablespoon tomato paste
1 bay leaf
6 ciabatta rolls, or 1 Italian loaf, sliced
5 ounces pancetta, chopped
1 medium onion, chopped
1 medium carrot, chopped
1 pound frozen spinach or kale, thawed and dried
15 ounces canned cannellini or navy beans
3 cups chicken stock
¼ cup extra virgin olive oil
Freshly grated parmesan cheese
Italian flat-leaf parsley, chopped
Sea salt and freshly ground black pepper to taste

In a large soup pot over medium heat, heat the olive oil. Add the minced garlic, chopped onion, carrot, pancetta, and salt and pepper to taste. Cook until the onion is golden brown and the pancetta is crispy, about 8 minutes.

Add the tomato paste and stir to mix well. Add tomatoes and stir. Scrape the bottom of the pan with a wooden spoon to release the brown bits. Add the beans, parsley stock, bay leaf, and pecorino cheese. Bring the soup to a boil, reduce heat, and simmer for 30 minutes.

Dip the ciabatta slices or the Italian loaf that has been cut into ¼" slices into the olive oil, coating both sides. Bake on a baking sheet in a 350° oven until golden brown; or, grill on a grill or fry pan.

Rub each piece of bread with the whole garlic clove (or you may choose to roast the garlic along with the bread in the oven and then spread onto the bread). Place each piece of bread in a soup bowl and pour the soup mix over it. Sprinkle with freshly grated pecorino cheese.

This is a special cut of meat from the region's Chianina breed of cattle, prized for their tenderness and flavor. I had mine served over a simple bed of baby arugula, with lemon slices and a glass of Brunello wine. Crusty garlic bread topped this dish off very nicely.

Bistecca alla Fiorentina - Tuscan Porterhouse
Serves 4. Prep time: 60 minutes.

2½ pound porterhouse steak, preferably Chianina
¼ cup Tuscan extra virgin olive oil
4 sprigs fresh rosemary, chopped fine
2 fresh lemons, cut into about 6 wedges
Sea salt and freshly ground black pepper

Marinate the steak at room temperature in the freshly ground rosemary for about 1 hour.

On an outdoor grill, use a hardwood charcoal such as hickory and heat until coals are white and hot.

Rub the olive oil onto the steak and coat well. Season with salt and black pepper. Place steak on the heated grill and cook until a dark golden brown crust forms, about 5 to 10 minutes depending upon the thickness of the steak. Turn the steak over and continue cooking the other side, 5 to 10 minutes more. Temperature inside should be about 125°. Take the steak off the grill and allow it to rest for about 10 minutes.

To serve, remove the two pieces of meat from the bone and replace the bone on a serving platter. Trim any unwanted fat from the round tenderloin steak. Slice into 6 equal pieces at an angle and fan out on one side of the bone. Slice into ¼" slices at an angle to the grain. Fan out on the other side of the bone. Serve on a plate with baby arugula and the lemon slices.

Sicily - This is the region Grandmother Grace's side of the family is from.

Occupations by the Greeks, Romans, Normans, Spanish, and French have left their culinary influence on the flavorful mix of foods from Sicily. The Arab influence brought the introduction of citrus, cumin, saffron, rice, almonds, pistachios, and sugar cane, to name just a few, as well as eggplant, which is used in some of my signature dishes.

One of my favorite vegetarian dishes is Pasta alla Norma. This dish is said to have been especially created in Catania, Sicily for the royalty at the time of Vincenzo Bellini, composer of the opera *Norma* which starred the world-famous soprano Maria Callas. This is a simple version, but you can be creative in the use of the ingredients.

Pasta alla Norma
Serves 4. Prep time: 40 minutes.

2 medium Italian eggplants, peeled or unpeeled, cut into 1" cubes
1 pound rigatoni pasta
3 cloves garlic, thinly sliced
15 large basil leaves
½ cup of red wine
1 pound peeled tomatoes, fresh or canned (plum tomatoes are good in this recipe)
7 ounces ricotta salata
Sea salt and freshly ground black pepper

In a large skillet with some olive oil, sauté the sliced garlic over medium high heat, being careful not to burn. Add the tomatoes, salt, pepper, and basil leaves, and red wine and simmer on low for 20 minutes.

In another skillet, add the rest of the olive oil – enough to cover the eggplant – and fry the cubed eggplant until golden brown and crispy. Remove to paper towels to drain.

Boil the rigatoni *al dente*. Drain, reserving a spoonful of the pasta water.

In a bowl, mix the tomato sauce with the pasta and coat well. Mix in the eggplant. Using a coarse cheese grater, grate the ricotta salata over the pasta and fried eggplant. Serve on a plate and garnish with a few basil leaves.

For the sweet tooth, there are the world-famous cannoli, cassata, and crushed ice with syrup toppings. Yes, pure culinary bliss!

Cannoli

Cannoli originated in Sicily and is said to have been influenced by the Arab culture. It was historically prepared during Carnevale season. My very first taste of this deep-fried, crunchy, cream-filled pastry was at my Grandmother Grace's house during the holidays. My first cannoli shell dipped in chocolate and filled with ricotta came when my mother, Ida, took me to the Feast of Saint Genaro, a well-attended Italian festival in New York City's "Little Italy" section, when I was a young boy. These are fond memories of one of my favorite desserts.

Cannoli Siciliana
Serves 24. Prep time: 30 minutes.

Special items needed:
Set of 4 - 5" long metal tubes, to wrap the dough around
4½" diameter cookie cutter

For the Cannoli Cream
3 cups whole milk Ricotta cheese, drained (use Ricotta Impastata if you can find it)
1/2 cup mini chocolate chips
1 1/2 cups confectioners' sugar
1 1/2 tsp. vanilla extract
1/4 cup granulated sugar
1/2 cup fresh whipped cream
2 small lemons, zested

In a medium bowl, beat the heavy cream until soft peaks are formed.

In another bowl, mix the drained ricotta with the sugar, chocolate chips, lemon zest, and confectioners' sugar. Fold in the whipped cream and let sit.

Just before filling the shells, place into a pastry bag.

For the Shells
1 3/4 cups all-purpose flour
1 tablespoon sugar

1/4 teaspoon kosher salt
1/4 cup red wine vinegar
3 tablespoons Marsala wine
2 tablespoons unsalted butter, melted and cooled to room temperature
1 large egg white, lightly beaten
Vegetable oil or grape seed oil for deep frying

In a medium bowl or mixer bowl, sift the flour, salt, and sugar. Mix with a fork the old-school way or an electric blender. If using an electric blender, put on the paddle and add the butter; blend well for 2 to 3 minutes, until it forms small bread crumbs texture. Or, mix well with the fork until you get the same consistency.

Add Marsala wine. Mix two to three minutes until the dough starts to come together and form a clump. Add more wine if needed.

Remove the dough ball from the bowl and knead with your hand on a clean surface until it is all together smooth. Wrap in plastic wrap and let it sit on the counter for about an hour.

In a deep pan or a fryer, heat oil to 360 degrees.

Unwrap the dough and cut a quarter of it off. Lightly flour the surface and roll it out with a rolling pin until it is very thin, almost translucent. Let sit for 10 minute so it relaxes.

With a ¼" round ring cutter (or bigger for larger shells), cut small circles from the dough. Roll each circle out until it is very thin and smooth. Wrap each circle of dough around a lightly oiled cannoli metal form until the ends touch. Dip your finger into the egg white and seal the dough together.

Gently, ease two or three dough wraps into hot oil, turning each a little so the bottom does not burn, for 45 seconds. Pick them up with tongs and slip each one off of the metal holders, letting them slide into the hot oil. They will float to the top. Take them out when they are a darker brown color and place them on a paper towel to dry. Let cool before filling.

With a pastry bag filled with cream, fill each side of the shells until the cream oozes out. If desired, dip each end in more chocolate chips or in crumbled pistachio nuts. Place on a plate and dust with confectioners' sugar.

Bologna

In the region of Bologna, tortellini is king. It can be filled with cheese, meat, fish, or vegetables. Traditionally, they are cooked with a simple chicken broth. Those who want to make the broth and the pasta from scratch can do that, but I have kept it simple by using ready-made ingredients. Enjoy!

Tortellini in *Brodo* (Simple broth)
Serves 6. Prep time: 20 minutes.

12 ounces tortellini pasta
16 ounces low-sodium chicken stock, box
16 ounces low-sodium beef stock, box
1 bay leaf
½ cup freshly grated pecorino cheese combination
Sea salt and freshly ground black pepper to taste

In a large soup pot, bring the chicken and beef stocks to a boil. Add the bay leaf and simmer for 10 minutes. Add the tortellini and cook al dente. Place in bowls and grate fresh cheese over the top. Add black pepper to taste.

Each note has the right to live.
~Arturo Toscanninni

Sing & Cook Bonus Section

Music: Our Sweetest Joy

"SONG IS MAN's sweetest joy," said the bard Musaeus, and Atheneauis reported in the second century that "it is no disgrace to confess that one knows nothing, but is it deemed a disgrace to decline to sing."

"Pure and bright as the sound of silver," said someone back in the sixteenth century who had just heard a *castrato* sing. Since much of the music at the time was written in the soprano range, and as women were not allowed in the church choirs, young boys with particularly beautiful voices would be castrated so that their voices wouldn't change at puberty. It was a popular way to give a man the soprano voice. I am, however, glad that the custom is no longer practiced!

The seventeenth and eighteenth centuries were characterized by several musical trends: the rise of the professional opera star, the wide popularity of the *castrato*, the development of the Italian style of singing known as *bel canto* (beautiful singing), and the cultivation of vocal ornamentation and artifice.

Singing as a Spiritual Experience

We sing with the mind, through the body. Tone flows out from the tonal center of consciousness as vibration. It is carried on the surface of the will, sustained but never forced by the will power. The vocal cords transform mental tone into physical sound. The will still controls the tone, through the physical medium of the breath. Breath does not create tone; it merely floats the tone as the physical carrier of the transformed mental impulse. That's why singing is a spiritual experience, and not simply a physical technique. The rule is: relax and sing, contract and bellow.

My Daily Singing Preparation

I enjoy going for a long bike ride into the mountains around Ojai, California, where I live. Each morning I take an eight mile journey up one of the many mountain paths that overlook the beautiful valley. I put my bike into an easy peddle gear and pump up the winding trails that snake around the orchards of oranges and avocados. Orange blossoms are one of the world's most intoxicating aromas.

I bike to a special place, a *piazza* at the top of a mountain, take out my pitch pipe, and sing my voice scales from low to high C. As I look over the valley, I'm transported to sunny Italy or Greece. The crystal-clear blue sky and golden glow of the sun burning off the fog below lends its own magic. This is when the beautiful Italian melodies come to me. As I hear myself sing, it seems my voice is coming through me, not from me. Each note, as clear as a bell, resonates and fills the valley with song. The smells of sage, lavender, and eucalyptus start my digestive juices flowing, and the magic starts to happen.

Music touches our emotions as no other form of communication can. Our inner emotional life is reflected in our physical surroundings, and singing can play an important and active part in creating whatever reality we desire in our lives. Like everyone, I want to fill my life with feelings of love and happiness, so I listen to and sing songs that feed those positive emotions in my life. When I sing, especially in Italian, I tap into those deep places in my heart that move my emotions and enable me to feel and experience the life force flowing through me, the feeling of being alive in that moment.

I've tapped into my ancestry deep in my DNA. When I sing Italian songs, there is something special and magical. I'm not just a singer singing songs. I become the song, and the emotion and passion flow through me.

Real Magic

What you are for empowers you.
What you are against weakens you.
~Dr. Wayne Dyer

In my life now, as I notice and observe the workings of the everyday thoughts and desires that fill my mind, I find one thing is certain: Nothing in this physical world ever remains the same. Everything is constantly changing. You must allow yourself to achieve a state of non-change each day to enable that creative energy to flow through you in the most effective way. It helps you grow and helps center the mind. It gives some depth to each and every day. It works for me.

My days start out with my meditation program, consisting of yoga *asanas*, *prana yama* (breathing technique), and a morning warm sesame oil self-massage. I sit quietly and practice a very ancient technique of mediation that allows me to tap into that place of non-change within myself. My best songs and recipes come to me at this time.

It doesn't matter what we've done in the past. The past doesn't equal the future, it is said. What's important is being alive every moment. That's one of the reasons I've decided to make no compromises with my happiness and well-being. We have the choice to manifest whatever we put our attention on. The more we serve from the place of true giving and caring for the world, the more we get back from it. It's a simple law of nature. Living life simply, with integrity and truthfulness, is all one can do to allow life to flow with little effort, like the river to the ocean.

Inspirational Sources

Almost everywhere you go throughout the Italian countryside, there's a melody that's playing in someone's heart. The patron saint of music is St. Cecilia. I wonder what her favorite pasta dish was.

A person who sings is a happy person. Singing allows us to open our hearts and communicate our deep emotions to the world through song. Melodies please the ears as, yes, those beautiful notes from a voice as smooth as silver that sends shivers up and downs your spine. That's what happens to me when I sing and when I hear some of the great singers. *Canzone* means "song" in Italian. A song of life.

I want to dedicate this chapter to some of the great classical singers, Italian and Swedish, who have moved people's hearts and souls through singing. "Immortal" is the way to describe them. Maybe you will be inspired to get some of their recordings, and sing along with them while you cook.

I keep a pitch pipe in my car (a C-to-C pitch) so I can tune up just about everywhere I go and sing to my heart's content. The next best thing to having a piano in your pocket, a pitch pipe is very portable.

Don't be afraid to open your lungs and sing out. It doesn't matter how it sounds or what anyone has told you in the past about the quality of your voice. Just do it for yourself. It's very magical and healing, and you'll enjoy it. Maybe you'll be delightfully surprised by what comes out of you. People tell me they sing only in the shower. If that's what it takes to get you to sing, then pretend you're in the shower while you're cooking, and go for it! Make every note count. Each breath breathes life into the notes, so give each and every note its full breath of life. Sing! Sing as if you were caressing every note.

The Grand Dame of Voice

The teachers of men drink their life from pure sources,
and take their message more directly from the soul of existence.
~Powell, 1925.

It was like a miracle meeting her. I had made a silent commitment to myself not to hide my talent for singing anymore. I wanted to manifest a teacher who had all the qualities I desired and needed. He or she had to able to teach me to sing in Italian, and at the same time, to understand it. I grew up with the traditional Neapolitan songs, but never really understood them. My teacher would need a lot of patience; and, of course, be within my budget.

Giovanna d'Onofrio was 89 years young, was born in a little town in Pennsylvania, and was world-traveled. She had studied in Rome. Her great uncle was a bishop and helped her take courses at a private school, though she never officially enrolled. I was introduced to her through a student of hers whom I met while getting a chiropractic adjustment. Right place, right time! Her family knew all the great singers in their heyday: Enrico Caruso, Beniamino Gigli, Eva Tetrazzini, and Mario Lanza. She traveled with some of them and picked up tips and age-old secrets. She had been through both world wars and knew a couple of popes and the world's wealthiest. The Hollywood studios hired her in the 1950-60s to heal and train some of the great voices. She was billed as a "voice constructionist."

D'Onofrio saved many voices that almost went under the surgeon's knife for polyps and sores. She knew that most singers just needed rest and instructions in breathing and how to use the full body. She was definitely a dying breed.

"The arias of the eighteenth century are seldom focused on anymore, for there are few singers who can do them justice," she said. According to her, there were too few teachers left who could teach.

"It's the vowels that sing in Italian," she once said. "The consonants are like a tennis racket: they propel forth the vowels into space. One cannot hold onto music, for it is not of this world. Once it is played or sung, it travels to another dimension."

Excitement and Italian are one word.
~Giovanna d'Onofrio

Italian Music Terms

A capella - without instrumental accompaniment
Adagio - slowly (between andante and largo)
Allegretto - not too fast (between andante and allegro)
Allegro - fast
Alto - lower range female voice (also called contralto)
Andante - moderate speed (between allegretto and adagio)
Aria - an elaborate composition for the solo voice
Arpeggio - notes of a chord sung or played one after another
Crescendo - from soft to loud (opposite is decrescendo)
Forte - loud
Tenor - the highest natural voice of a male
Soprano - the highest range for a female voice
Sostenuto - sustaining the tone to or beyond its nominal value
Piano - soft
Pianissimo - very soft
Pianissimo forte - from soft to loud

The Joy of Singing and Cooking

Yes, it's true! If music is the language of the heart, then food is the stuff of the soul. The glue that binds us all together. No matter where we come from and what we are brought up with, both food and music have influenced and are continuing to influence our lives each and every day.

Our basic needs are met by them. Our "hunger" for life is very real. Since times immemorial, the human race has traveled the world in search of food. I know because I have my favorite places to eat that I go to wherever I travel to another country or even another city.

Empires and civilizations were built around food and the knowledge of cooking it and its preparation and effect on the senses. Its preparation has been shared above and beyond the boundaries of each country, enabling us to have one world language. To eat with passion is to truly love. Watch what happens when you are with your family and friends when you cook a special ethnic dish, and you put some music on that relates to whatever you're cooking and eating.

The question arises, do we eat to live or do we live to eat? Just ask anyone in my family and it would seem that the latter is the gospel truth. As the tale of Odysseus states, "Tell me what you eat and I will tell you what you are" (if this were true then I would be a good bowl of pasta!); and the saying "we are what we eat" would also ring true. Gastronomy – the art and science of delicate eating – can become a religion if we allow it to. So can the music that we listen to before, during, and after the feast.
In my travels all over the world as The Singing Chef®, I have become convinced of one thing: we all need each other to help keep this great planet on which we live abundant with food and music for many generations to come. To sing, eat, and celebrate life every day is a great gift!

The following pages contain songs that go with special foods and menus. You can listen to samples of these songs by going to http://www.SingingChef.com/Audio.

SONGS AND RECIPES TO SING WHILE YOU COOK
From *Cooking Cabaret* CD, recorded January 2001

Food, Food, Glorious Food
To the tune of *Tarantella*

Everybody come with us, we're going to cook up a tasty treat;
Filled with flavor, smells divine, it's gonna knock you off of your feet.
Yeah, food, glorious food, we got delicious, delectable food,
And all you need is your appetite to put you in the right mood.

We've got Mediterranean, Mexican, Indian, Chinese, Japanese, Thai;
We cook Cajun, Caribbean, Latin American, anything under the sky.
We are chopping and dicing, sautéing and spicing, and frying 'til golden brown,
And we're baking and broiling, roasting and toasting, and grilling all over town.

Yeah, food, glorious food, it's incredible, edible stuff;
Three meals a day, at home or away, we can't seem to get enough.
Yeah, food, glorious food, invite all your family and friends;
The oven is warm, we'll cook up a storm, the fun never seems to end.

We're gonna start with an appetizer, and some bubbly French champagne,
Pass around the cheese and crackers, with spicy olives in top.
We like to set a dinner table with some linen and fine china,
Light the candles, add the flowers, and our favorite bottle of wine.

A chardonnay, a vin rose, merlot and zinfandel,
Sangiovese, cabernet, a fine brunello would be swell.
We're gonna drink and eat and sing until our spirits start to soar;
Raise our glasses to the sky, and then we'll all go back for more.

Food, food, glorious food, delicious, delectable food.
All you need is your appetite to put you in the mood.
Food, food, glorious food, what more can anyone say,
Just celebrate and fill up your plate; each day is a holiday.

Food, food, glorious food (repeat 3 times).

Sing & Cook Italian

The first knowledge of the Italian ricotta cake dates back to the Arabic domination of Sicily in Palermo. They introduced sugarcane, bitter orange, lemon, lime, mandarin, and almond. All these foods, together with ricotta that has been produced in Sicily from the prehistoric times, were the ingredients of this Italian ricotta cake. My recipe has been Americanized to keep it simple, so that everyone who tries it succeeds.

The story of polenta, known as Italian grits to some, goes back many years in history. The people in the south of Italy got most of their energy from pasta, and the northern folks would eat daily polenta. Since Roman times, this grain, or porridge, was served as a peasant food, called cucina povera in Italian. Now you can find it in the best gourmet restaurants all over the world, served in many ways. Polenta is white or golden-yellow, depending on how it is milled. In Italy, from Veneto to Sicily it is served with fish, beef, pork, veal, and wild boar to add texture and smooth flavor.

On the next page is the song to sing while making Nonna's Ricotta Cheesecake, and Polenta. Listen to this song, and the following songs, at http://www.SingingChef.com/Audio. Have fun!

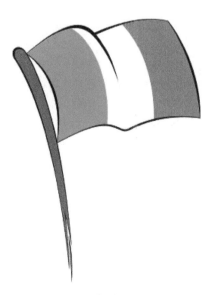

Sing & Cook Italian
To the tune of *Funiculi-Funicula*

Today we're going to sing and cook Italian—
Come on along, and have some fun.
Oh yeah, we're gonna make ricotta cake
For everyone, for everyone!

We start with all the right ingredients, the oven's on 350 heat.
And now we're getting ready to begin, in a bowl we're mixing in,
Six eggs, vanilla, a cup of sugar please, a half a cup of flour, and fresh ricotta cheese.
And don't forget the chocolate chips, the chocolate chips, the chocolate chips.

Mix it all and bake and there you have Ricotta Cake.
Mix it all and bake and there you have Ricotta Cake.

And now we're gonna make one polenta—
A corn meal dish, it's good with fish,
Topped with cheese, roasted peppers and some mushrooms,
Whatever you wish, what a dish!

Bring four cups of water to a boil, and add some salt, and pepper too,
Some milk will make it oh, so nice and creamy, we'll leave it all up to you.
One cup corn meal, some butter garlic too,
Add one bay leave and all that's left to do
is take your spoon and then you stir, and then your stir, and then your stir!

For fifteen minutes more and in a baking pan you'll pour;
Well, any more than that, you'll have to throw it out the door,
Well, any more than that, you can roll it in a ball,
Any more than that, you can bounce it off the wall!

When it cools, cut into little squares; fry it, grill it, serve it up with flare.
So there you have the recipes; serve them to your family!

It's been so much fun to sing and cook Italian;
It's been so much fun to sing and cook Italian!

Sing & Cook French
To the tune of the *Can-Can*

Cooking French today, we're cooking French, making crepes, yeah, light and tasty crepes.
Cooking French today, we're cooking French, making crepes so many different ways.

First we heat the frying pan, then we put the butter in, butter in the frying pan, yeah, oh, oh.
Cooking French today, we're cooking French, follow us, yeah, now we'll show you how.

Whisk eggs and flour in a bowl, then add a cup of fresh whole milk, some vanilla, sugar too; a pinch of salt will do.

Let sit for thirty minutes more, then a quarter cup of batter, pour into the pan, cook till brown, flip over, put on plate.

Fill with sautéed vegetables, roll up with some sauce and ham,
spoon inside fresh cottage cheese, serve them with strawberry jam;

fold inside some lemon curd, dust with powdered sugar and
melted chocolate, roll up tight; you'll savor every bite.

Now everyone will dance and sing your praises when they taste your crepes;
Oui, oui, just like in gay Paris, oh yes.

Serve them with some French champagne, green salad on the plate, and then it's time to celebrate.

Well every day's a holiday, yes, when you sing and cook this way, all your friends will jump for joy, they'll say *merci beaucoup*!

Bon appetit to everyone; yes, cooking French is so much fun! (Repeat.)

From hot croissants, to soufflés light, cooking French is out of sight!

French Crepes

Crepes originated in Brittany in the northwest region of France. They were originally called *galettes*. Crepes are popular not only in France but elsewhere in Europe, where they are given other names. The Italians call them *crespelle*; Jewish people know them as *blintzes*; in Scandinavia they are *plattars*; Russians call them *blini*, and in Greece they are *krepes*.

They can be filled with sweet fillings like fresh cut fruit, lemon curd, Nutella, or strawberry jam, as well as savory fillings like cheese, pulled pork, sour cream, spinach, beans, sautéed vegetables, or many other tasty things.

Here are some of my favorite French recipes that you can sing the ingredients to while you cook.

Sweet and Savory Crepes
Serves 14. Prep time: 40 minutes.

1¾ cups unbleached all-purpose flour
¾ teaspoon sea salt
1½ cups milk
1 tablespoon sugar
3 large, fresh eggs
2 tablespoons clarified butter or ghee
1½ sticks unsalted butter

Sift the flour and salt together into a bowl and make a well in the center. Add 1¼ cups of the milk and the sugar and gradually whisk the flour into it. Add the eggs one at a time, whisking just until blended. Then whisk in the remaining liquid. Let sit for about 30 minutes.

Heat a 10" crepe pan over medium-high heat; brush with clarified butter.

Using a ¼ cup measure, pour the batter into the center of the pan. Quickly turn and shake the pan until the batter coats the bottom. Let cook until the crepe is golden brown and beginning to curl at the edges, about 1½ minutes.

Gently pull the crepe up using a wooden spoon or plastic spatula, and turn it over until done, about 30 seconds.

Repeat with the rest of the butter and the batter.

Choose your savory or sweet fillings to roll into the crepes.

For savory crepes:
1½ cups small-curd cottage cheese, seasoned with paprika or your favorite savory spice
1 cup chopped cremini mushrooms, sautéed
1 cup chopped and sautéed mixed vegetables, such as zucchini, eggplant, and spinach
2 to 3 slices black forest ham, thinly sliced

Or, for sweet crepes:
½ cup strawberry jam, or 1 cup chopped fresh strawberries
½ cup lemon curd
½ cup Italian mascarpone cheese
½ cup cherry jam
½ cup apricot jam
1 cup chocolate sauce
1 cup of your favorite nuts – walnuts, peanuts, pecans, cashews, etc.

Sing & Cook with Andy LoRussso

Sing & Cook Mexicana
Sung to the tunes of *Cielito Linda*, *Jarabe Tapatio*, *La Cucaracha*

Ai, Yai, Yai, Yai! Sing and cook Mexicana!
In a hot iron skillet, heat vegetable oil, cook fresh white fish until golden,
Break up in bite size pieces, and in a warm tortilla we'll fold in,
Shredded up fennel, some sharp yellow cheeks, green loins and chili powder,
Just add some red hot salsa, guaranteed to make your eyes water.

Ai, Yai, Yai, Sing & cook Mexicana,
we made some fence fish tacos and now we'll cook up some frijoles.
Making *frijoles*, tasty *frijoles*, *frijoles,* melted cheese, and rice,
Making *frijoles* tasty *frijoles*, *frijoles* sure to be so nice.

Soak two cups of pinto beans in warm water overnight, drain,
replace the liquid, slowly simmer, cover tight.
Add a sliced white onion, garlic and some bacon diced,
cook two or three more hours, the aroma will entice.

Serve them as a side dish, cook them into refried beans,
As a topping for tostadas, mix in cheese and sour cream
Add some cayenne pepper, make a spicy chili pot,
but please don't burn the house down, 'cause your chili is to hot!

Now in an oiled saucepan, add a quarter cup of rice,
cook until it's golden,
about five minutes will suffice.

Add the diced red pepper, green onion and tomato paste,
Cilantro and the garlic, and then you season it to taste ,
Add two cups of water, cook for twenty minute more,
Over a low simmer, they'll be banging down your door!

Making *frijoles*, tasty *frijoles*, *frijoles,* melted cheese, and rice,
Making *frijoles*, tasty *frijoles*, and they turned out very nice,
they taste so good they're going fast!
It's been a total gas!

A few of my favorite Mexican/Spanish singer/performers are Selena, Linda Ronstadt, Los Lobos, Jose Feliciano, and Julio Iglesias.

Here are some of my favorite Mexican recipes that you can sing the ingredients to while you cook.

Fennel Fish Tacos

It is estimated that the first known tacos originated in the 1500s. The simplicity of the taco makes it food that almost everyone can make for little money. The ability to add a number of meats like chicken, beef, or pork, as well as steak, and toppings like lettuce, avocado, tomatoes, salsa, and guacamole, make it a simple, world-wide sensation that all cultures can enjoy.
Serves 6. Prep time: 30 minutes.

6 flour tortillas
1 pound firm, fresh white fish, such as snapper, rockfish, or sea bass
2 tablespoons lime juice
½ cup green onions, chopped
3 tablespoons vegetable or canola oil
Salt, freshly ground pepper, and chili powder to taste
1 cup shredded fennel (anise)
1 cup sharp cheddar cheese, shredded

If using packaged tortillas, wrap them tightly with foil and place in preheated 350° oven for 15 to 20 minutes, or until warmed through. Grill the tortillas if you are making them fresh.

Rinse the fish with cold water and pat dry. Rub lime juice over the surface of the fish; sprinkle with salt and pepper.

Heat a large cast-iron skillet over high heat until almost smoking, about 7 minutes. Add the vegetable oil, then the fish. Cook two or three minutes on each side, or until golden. Sprinkle with some more lime juice and break into bite-sized pieces.

Place the fish in the center of a warm tortilla and top with fennel, cheese, and green onions. Sprinkle with chili powder. Fold in half and serve on a warm plate with sour cream, guacamole, and frijoles with melted cheese.

Frijoles with Melted Cheese

Frijoles are a dish of cooked and mashed beans that is a traditional staple of Mexican and Tex-Mex cooking. The pinto bean is the most popular and is most often used for this dish. One can also use black beans or red kidney beans.
Serves 6-8 (makes 4 cups). Prep time: 40 minutes.

2 cups dried pinto beans
1 white onion, halved and sliced
1 garlic clove, minced
8 ounces bacon, diced
¼ teaspoon cayenne pepper
1 cup shredded cheddar or Monterey jack cheese
Salt to taste

Pick over beans to remove any stones.

Place the beans in a large pot, add water to cover by 2 inches, and soak overnight.

Rinse and drain the beans; put back in the pot with the onion, garlic and, bacon. Add water to cover by 1 inch. Bring to a boil; lower heat and simmer for 2-3 hours, until the beans are tender and most of the liquid is absorbed. Add salt to taste. Mash well. Mix in one cup of shredded cheese.

Traditional Mexican Rice

Rice was introduced to Mexico from the Philippines via Acapulco. The type of rice used is usually the long grain rice, but Rick Bayless, one of my favorite cooks of traditional Mexican food, recommends medium-grained white rice for best results.
Serves 6. Prep time: 40 minutes.

¼ cup long-grain white rice
2½ cups cold water
½ cup red bell pepper, diced
¼ cup onion, finely chopped
¼ cup fresh cilantro, minced
¼ cup vegetable oil
⅓ cup tomato paste (puree)
2 garlic cloves, minced
Salt to taste

Heat oil in a large, heavy saucepan over medium heat. Add rice and stir until the rice is golden (about 5 minutes). Add the red pepper and onion and cook another 5 minutes.

Reduce the heat; add cilantro, tomato paste and garlic. Mix well.

Add water and salt; raise heat and bring to a boil. Cover tightly and reduce heat to low; simmer for 20-30 minutes, or until the water is absorbed.

Remove from heat and let sit for 10 minutes before serving.

Sing & Cook Irish
Sung to the tunes of *Tura Lura Lura, When Irish Eyes are Smiling, The Irish Jig*

Tura Lura Lura, Tura Lura Lu,
There's nothing that warms the heart,
Like my grandmothers Irish stew.

Tura Lura Lura, Tura Lura Lu, in an eight quart kettle
We're cooking up some scrumptious Irish Stew.

Add four cups of chicken broth, simmer lamb some parsley and thyme,
Cover for an hour or more, the aroma will be divine.

Add potatoes, carrots, and onions, chopped up celery more broth too,
Cook about an hour or more, while your drinking your favorite brew.

Pass the sauerkraut and corned beef, there's something that can be said.
We've only just begun to eat now we'll make some soda bread.

In a bowl, mix the flour, baking powder and soda too,
Work the butter and the shortening in, a pinch of salt will do.

Add the egg and buttermilk, gently knead into a ball,
Place it on a greased cookie sheet you can hear the oven call.

Cook till golden brown and dance around, about forty minutes or so,
Then you'll be in Irish heaven, when you take a bit you'll know.

May the road rise up to meet you, as you sing this merry song,
With our Irish stew and soda bread, we know you can't go wrong!

Some of my favorite Irish singers are Van Morrison, Enya, and Bono for contemporary music; and John McCormak, Celine Byrne, and any of the Celtic Woman singers for opera.

Following are some of my favorite Irish recipes that you can sing the ingredients to while you cook.

Traditional Irish Stew

Irish stew – or in Gaelic, *ballymaloe* – typically contains chunks of lamb or mutton, potatoes, onion, parsley, and sometimes carrots. Considered a peasant dish due to its humble roots, it is known all over the world and is a traditional Irish comfort food. Serves 10. Prep time: 40 minutes.

3 pounds boneless lamb shoulder, trimmed and cut into one inch pieces
1½ tablespoons fresh parsley, minced
1 teaspoon dried thyme, crumbled
6 cups chicken broth
3 pounds boiling potatoes, peeled and quartered
1 large onion, finely chopped
1 pound carrots, peeled and cut into ½" pieces
6 stalks celery, trimmed and ribs cut into ½" pieces
6 tablespoons all-purpose flour
¼ cup vegetable oil

In an 8-quart kettle, simmer lamb, parsley, and thyme, covered, in chicken broth for about two hours. Season with salt and pepper to taste.

Add potatoes, onion, carrots, celery, and remaining two cups of broth. Simmer, covered, for one more hour.

In a small bowl, whisk together flour and oil until smooth; stir into simmering stew until well incorporated. Simmer stew uncovered until it is thickened, three to five more minutes.

Irish Soda Bread

Irish soda bread is a traditional product of a poor country. It was made with basic ingredients: flour, baking soda instead of yeast, soured milk, and salt. Before baking, a cross was cut on the top with a knife to ward off the devil and protect the household. It is shaped in different shapes based on the region of Ireland in which it is being prepared. The traditional service of the bread is for a section to be broken off, then split and buttered while it is warm.
Serves 10. Prep time: 40 minutes.

2 cups all-purpose flour
2 teaspoons baking powder
1 teaspoon baking soda
½ teaspoon salt
2 tablespoons unsalted butter
2 tablespoons vegetable shortening
1 egg, beaten
1 cup buttermilk

Preheat the oven to 375°.

In a large bowl, combine the flour, baking powder and baking soda and salt and mix well.

Cut the butter and the shortening into small pieces and add to the flour mixture until it resembles coarse crumbs.

Add the egg and the buttermilk and mix into the flour mixture until it is all incorporated.

Turn the dough out onto a floured surface and knead gently until the dough forms a smooth ball.

Form into a 12 inch loaf and place the loaf on a lightly greased cookie sheet and into the oven to bake for about forty to forty five minutes or until golden brown.

Sing & Cook Jewish
Sung to the tune of *Hava Nagila*

Matzahs we're making, matzahs we're making,
matzahs we're making, momma's matzah balls.

Have some, you've got to have some,
I'm getting hungry for momma's mean matzah balls.

She made the chicken soup, we've got the chicken fat,
come and cook along with us; you'll love every bite.

When you're feeling blue, momma she'll tell you to
Mix up a batch of them, it cures everything.

Mix up, mix up, mix up.
Mix eggs with chicken fat, mix in matzah meal and salt.

Add some chicken soup and stir,
chill in fridge for forty minutes
then take out, then take out, and roll into little balls.

Boil in salt water for about forty minutes more,
then drop them in the soup, you'll sing *mazel tov*.

Serve them with gefilte fish, fried latkes out on a dish,
Blintzes with cottage cheese, chopped up liver on rye.

Challah, challah, challah,
Pass the bagels and some lox,
sour cream and ungahocks.

Fry pirogues in some onions.
Call the doctor, oy! my bunions.

Sing l'chaim Sing l'chaim
My shayna maydala.

This is my favorite way to make matzah balls and chicken soup.

Matzah Balls and Chicken Soup

Matzah balls are an Ashkenazi Jewish soup dumpling made from a mixture of matzah meal, eggs, water, and fat, such as oil or chicken fat (called *schmaltz*). The more eggs and fat in proportion to matzah meal, the lighter the matzah balls. They are served in chicken soup especially around Passover time, but you can enjoy them whenever you feel the need for a good comfort food.

The traditional chicken soup is the real Jewish penicillin. It is often served on Jewish holidays such as Rosh Hashanah and Yum Kippur. Many folks love this soup as it brings back memories of mother at home taking care of you.
Serves 6. Prep time: 60 minutes.

Making the Chicken Soup

1 whole, 5-pound, Kosher chicken, cut into 8 pieces
1 pound chicken wings, necks, or backs
2 large yellow onions, unpeeled, quartered
6 celery stalks cut into 1" pieces
4 large carrots, peeled, cut into 1" pieces
1 large shallot, quartered
1 bulb of garlic, halved crosswise
1 tablespoon black peppercorns

Bring all ingredients and 12 cups water to a boil in a very large pot.

Reduce heat to medium-low and simmer until chicken is cooked through, about 20 minutes.

Let cool slightly, then remove meat and return bones to stock.

Shred meat; wrap tightly and chill.

Continue to simmer stock until reduced by a third, about two hours more.

Strain chicken stock through a large mesh sieve. You should have about 8 cups.

Making the Matzah Balls

3 eggs, beaten to blend
¾ cup matzah meal
¼ cup *schmaltz* (chicken fat)
3 tablespoons club soda
1¼ teaspoons kosher salt

Mix all ingredients in a medium bowl. Cover and chill. It will firm up in about 2 hours.

To cook, bring chicken stock back to a boil in a large saucepan. Add carrots and salt. Reduce heat and simmer until carrots are tender, about 7 minutes. Add breast meat and cover.

Meanwhile, bring a large pot of well-salted water to a boil. Scoop out two tablespoon portions of the matzah ball mixture and form into small balls with your hands. Add matzah balls to the simmering water. Cover pot and cook though until they start to sink, about 20 to 25 minutes.

Transfer balls to bowls, about three in each (or if a large size ball, one in each bowl). Ladle some soup over the matzah balls. Garnish with dill and season with kosher salt and black pepper to taste.

The truest expression of a people is in its dance and music. ~Agnes de Mile

Testimonials

Testimonial from people I've had the privilege to work with:

In 1997, ANDY and I met performing together at one of the largest Italian festivals in the USA. When he cooks and sings, he brings out the best of his heart and soul in his Italian heritage.
~Tony Gemignani, 12 time World Pizza Champion, cookbook author, owner of 17 restaurants, tonygemegnani.com

Andy, The Singing Chef®, is one of the most unique chefs in the business. As a regular guest of my restaurant, he always has a kind word and an insightful tip for me. I've known many passionate chefs throughout my career but none so spirited about their work that the only way they know how to express it is through song. Bravo, Chef!
~Joe Baumel, Chef and co-owner of The Persona Pizza Franchise, PersonPpizza.Com

I've had the pleasure of working alongside Chef LoRusso, and his sense of personal style and ability to entertain are second to none. His passion for food and music are apparent in all he does.
~Richard Fisher, Executive Chef

The idea that Andy can transport so many back to his childhood kitchen – the feeling and richness of one's cultural upbringing – warms the heart.
~Brad Sherman, Restaurant owner, musician

Andy's brilliance comes from his ability to talk a room filled with strangers and make them all feel like family by the end of the night. As he prepares his family recipes, he sings his way into everybody's hearts. There is so much joy and gratitude in his performance, and it is contagious!
~Anna Lopez-Car & Donatella Lopez-Le Sorelle, www.lesorelleimports.com.

Chef LoRusso did an amazing job as chef and singer to my staff. He amazed them with a wonderful pasta creation while entertaining them with song and music. He got them so motivated hearing his stories and singing along with him. He has a fantastic talent of involving the audience during his performance.
~Joe Edem, CEC AAC, Executive Chef at Regional Medical Center in Reno, NV

I met Andy, The Singing Chef®, at a special event at the Junction City, Kansas, Opera House, where he was the featured Celebrity Chef. During the show, the audience and everyone was absolutely captivated by him. Working as his sous-chef, I took home more than on-the-job training – a friendship that would last a lifetime. Thanks for the opportunity, Andy; it has been my privilege and honor.
~Joe Font, Chef, Caterer

It was a pleasure cooking with my Italian stallion brother at the Mill Casino in Oregon. Andy had the ladies drooling over his good looks and left the cooking for me, his primo sous-chef for the VIP show. Tons of fun. Let's do it again soon!
~Dan Catanio, Executive Chef

Andy LoRusso is the amazing Italian chef who sings.
Never will the Bristol, Virginia Paramount Theater forget the joy he brings.
Delightful was the music and delicious the menu. Thank
You, Andy, for joining us afterwards for dinner at the Virginian Golf Club venue.
~Etta Nicewonder, The Nicewonder Group, www.thevirginian.com

There is nothing like the experience of having Andy in your kitchen. He not only demonstrates the masterful cooking of iconic Italian dishes, but also the Italian way of life encompassing more than cooking. It is about enjoyment, laughter, and making connections. Thank you, Andy, for the magical evenings!
~Jim and Tina Aho, Aho-Aho Consulting Inc.

Testimonials

Working with Andy LoRusso, The Singing Chef®, was one of the best entertainment, singing and cooking concert shows. I had the pleasure to be the PR photographer at his venues. A great talent and gentleman.
~Darrell Westmoreland, Photographer of the Stars

Chef Andy LoRusso is a unique talent who has merged together the art of cuisine and singing like no one before. His passion and traditional Italian roots are selected in every song he performs and every dish he creates. With his craft he truly understands how to touch all of your five senses.
~Asif Rasheed Syed, Chef/Owner of 21 Spices in Naples, FL, 21spicesdining.com

We had so much fun seeing Chef Andy cook, but most of all enjoyed his singing and interacting with all the patrons of our restaurant. We cannot wait for his return.
~Anji Harvard, Capa-Marka

Testimonials from some of the great people who have attended my shows:

I wanted to drop a quick note on a truly enjoyable dining experience for my family and board members at Lundberg Family Farms on May 30th. We enjoyed the singing, the views of Italy, and the special attention you paid to creating something delicious from our family of rice products.
~Grant Lundberg (Read full letter on my website, www.SingingChef.com)

…mix pop and jazz technique which makes an interesting and unique sound…mix flavors in your singing style, like you do with your cooking!
~From WFBL 1390 Radio Hosts Joey and Jim, Syracuse, NY

Received your CD and am so thrilled you autographed it for me! I bought your book and tape many years ago and wore it out… You are SO CHARISMATIC. Feeling blessed with your music.
~Carla

I do want to thank you for such a fabulous job last night… Great working with you, you're a true gem at what you do.
~Tina

…absolute genius. Stick at the festival circuit and you will achieve cult status. There may not have been the biggest crowd, but lots of people were digging your set. Great work!
~Ian

I have attended hundreds of Spencer shows over the years and yours by far just became my favorite! The Spencer Theater is a very special place and you did it justice with your singing and fabulous food.
~Katie

…you were fantastic! Quite possibly the highlight of the festival for me, far more entertaining than anything on the main stage!
~Alex

I hope that something comes of the *Grillin' and Chillin'*, that song was amazing!
~Tim

…fantastic double appearance at the Isle of Wight festival. You were absolutely fantastic and after watching your first appearance, my friend and I couldn't resist coming to the Saturday show and encouraging many others who all shared our appreciation for your talents.
~Dan, New UK Fan

…watch your show in the Big Top on Saturday and thought it was lovely, really enjoyed singing *That's Amore* with you!!! …thank you for being a stellar artist and an all-round lovely guy! It has been a pleasure.
~Clare

Andy LoRusso is one of the most talented and unique individuals that I have ever had the pleasure to know…impressed by Andy's talent, ability to connect with his audience and beautiful voice.
~Liz

…we have received nothing but great feedback from the property and its guests about your show. They said the guests will be talking about your show for months to come. AWESOME JOB!
~David

I…discovered your single *The Great Magic of Love* and *Dancing Master*. I absolutely love the songs… *The Great Magic of Love*, in particular, is one of those songs that always makes me smile and makes me want to get up and dance every time I hear it!
~Chris Rouse

Index

Index

Index

CPSIA information can be obtained
at www.ICGtesting.com
Printed in the USA
BVHW012135141118
533183BV00001B/1/P